PAINTING
Nature

discover the delightful details of nature

PAINTING
Nature

discover the delightful details of nature

PEGGY HARRIS

NORTH LIGHT BOOKS

CINCINNATI, OHIO
www.artistsnetwork.com

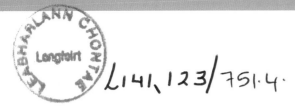
Library of Congress Cataloging-in-Publication Data

Harris, Peggy
  Painting nature / Peggy Harris.
       p. cm.
  Includes index.
  ISBN 1-58180-360-5 (alk. paper) -- ISBN 1-58180-715-5 (pbk. : alk. paper)
  1. Nature in art. 2. Painting--Technique. I. Title.
  ND1460.N38H37 2005
  751.4--dc22
                              2004024900

Editor: Holly Davis
Designer: Camille DeRhodes
Layout Artist: Amy F. Wilkin
Production Coordinator: Kristen Heller
Photographer: Christine Polomsky

Metric Conversion Chart

to convert	to	multiply by
Inches	Centimeters	2.54
Centimeters	Inches	0.4
Feet	Centimeters	30.5
Centimeters	Feet	0.03
Yards	Meters	0.9
Meters	Yards	1.1
Sq. Inches	Sq. Centimeters	6.45
Sq. Centimeters	Sq. Inches	0.16
Sq. Feet	Sq. Meters	0.09
Sq. Meters	Sq. Feet	10.8
Sq. Yards	Sq. Meters	0.8
Sq. Meters	Sq. Yards	1.2
Pounds	Kilograms	0.45
Kilograms	Pounds	2.2
Ounces	Grams	28.3
Grams	Ounces	0.035

About the Author

Author Peggy Harris is widely recognized for her trademark techniques for painting realistic fur and feathers and for her endearing portrayals of baby animals and birds.

Now, in *Painting Nature*, Peggy shares her techniques for painting a broader range of natural forms. Whether flowers or fish, cattails or crickets, twigs or toads, all reflect the artist's love and awe of her subject and her desire to help expand the artistic capabilities of her readers.

Peggy received her art training at the University of Kansas. She is a professional designer, international teacher and author of multiple books and magazine articles. Peggy's North Light Books titles, *Painting Baby Animals with Peggy Harris* and *Painting Baby Animal Treasures*, along with her five instructional DVDs and video tapes, have helped thousands of painters realize their dream of painting animals.

Peggy and her husband, Bob Sanders, live outside Nashville, Tennessee, in the wooded hills that are home to many of the plants and creatures featured in this book.

Contact information:
3848 Martins Chapel Road
Springfield, TN 37172
www.peggyharris.com

DEDICATION

For my dear friend, North Light
Books Acquisitions Editor,
Kathy Kipp, without whose
faith and help this book
would have been impossible.

Table of CONTENTS

Introduction

ALTHOUGH I AM KNOWN PRIMARILY AS AN ANIMAL ARTIST, I HAVE WANTED FOR SOME TIME TO WRITE A BOOK FEATURING OTHER SUBJECTS IN NATURE.

Many of my readers and students have indicated that they would like to include more skillfully rendered elements from nature in their animal paintings but feel intimidated by these subjects.

Others yearn to paint photorealistic nature vignettes but feel overwhelmed by the details and are uncertain how even to begin.

Some simply want a one-source reference book of common plants and creatures to assist them in painting nature in their own designs and in their own style.

This book is for each of you to use in your own way as you progress in your artistic journey.

BON VOYAGE!

Peggy Harris

My Objective

IF YOU HAVE THE DESIRE TO PAINT NATURE, THE APPROACH, TECHNIQUES AND AIDS DESCRIBED IN THIS BOOK MAKE YOUR GOAL EASIER TO ACCOMPLISH THAN YOU MIGHT HAVE SUPPOSED.

My aim is to acquaint you with the inexhaustible diversity that occurs in nature and thus expand your perception and available choices of subject. As you carefully examine and compare subjects from the natural world, you will inevitably become more skilled in your depiction of them.

Although the illustrations in this book cannot be considered totally faithful anatomical or botanical renderings, I have attempted to remain true to the essence of each subject. Distinctive characteristics and significant details play an important role in even the most simplistic representation of a subject. It is my intent that by calling attention to these traits, you will be able to paint the subject better, no matter what medium you choose or style you employ, from cartoon to photorealism.

Scientific names—and sometimes even common names—for subjects in this book have been omitted. This promotes contemplative observation of the variety and intricacy of subjects within a plant or animal group as opposed to automatic labeling, and resulting dismissal, of individual examples.

Painting instruction is confined mainly to the opening chapters, since the skills and techniques used are not difficult to master and do not vary significantly from page to page or subject to subject. Each section provides at least one step-by-step progression, which may be used as a model for painting other subjects in that section.

THIS IS PRIMARILY A BOOK TO TRAIN YOUR EYE RATHER THAN YOUR HAND—A PICTURE BOOK, IF YOU WILL, PRESENTED WITH THE KNOWLEDGE THAT ART BEGINS IN OUR HEARTS, IS ONLY AS GOOD AS OUR EYES AND FLOWS THROUGH, RATHER THAN IS CREATED BY, OUR HANDS.

Learning to See

IF YOU CANNOT PAINT A SUBJECT TO YOUR SATISFACTION, IT IS USUALLY DUE TO THE FACT THAT YOU HAVE NOT YET SEEN IT ACCURATELY.

We tend to paint what we subjectively assume we know of a subject, not what we objectively see. Worse yet, our brain abbreviates this "knowledge," distilling it to the bare minimum. The more complicated the subject, the more the brain takes for granted. The result? Our painting is a jumble of faulty assumptions in contrast to what we're actually seeing. We either convince ourselves that what we painted is what we had in mind or we find ourselves dissatisfied with our interpretation but uncertain how to improve our work.

While some painters seem to see more effortlessly than others, seeing is a learned skill. Enlisting the processes and aids discussed below will result in truly amazing strides in your ability to see, and thus paint, more skillfully.

A good selection of **RESOURCE PHOTOGRAPHS** of the subject, other than the art or photograph from which you are working, is essential. A single reference does not provide enough auxiliary information about a subject. When possible, obtain a real **SPECIMEN**. This is more valuable than any photograph.

An **ENLARGED COLOR PRINT** of your subject, matching the size you are painting, is also a powerful tool for success. Important information is less likely to get lost in translation. A **BLACK-AND-WHITE COPY** of this enlargement will reveal subtle value changes you may miss in the color copy.

A **MAGNIFYING GLASS** helps in studying photographic and specimen details as well as in checking your own painting for clarity and interpretation. I recommend a Magnabrite magnifier.

Occasionally viewing your work through a **CLEAR ACETATE COPY OF YOUR PATTERN** allows you to see more easily inadvertent form changes that may be occurring as you paint.

Sometimes tracing over the original photo or art helps you to mentally reinforce the correct shape or line. This phenomenon is known as **MUSCLE MEMORY,** since frequently the muscles can remember what the brain cannot. This is best done with the brush or tool you'll be using to execute the shape or line.

TRADITIONAL TRICKS such as looking at your work in a mirror or upside down, or checking the negative spaces or shapes (shapes you are delineating or revealing, but not painting) can also have merit.

ISOLATION WINDOWS (described on page 11) are perhaps the single greatest self-teaching aid a painter can use and are invaluable for developing your skills.

Isolation Windows

ISOLATION WINDOWS ARE "MAGIC GLASSES" THAT TRAIN OUR BRAIN AND EYE TO FOCUS ON ONE AREA AT A TIME. They help us see better by isolating a small area from its surroundings and forcing our eye to observe that area more accurately. Once we truly see our subject, it's much easier to paint.

making isolation windows

Using a very sharp X-Acto knife, simultaneously cut a hole or "window" in the center of two identical cards placed one on top of the other. Cut sets with windows of ¼" (6mm), ½" (13mm) and ¾"(19mm) for viewing and comparing different size areas. Sets with larger windows may be made if and when needed. If working from art or photos smaller or larger than your own work, cut proportional windows that reveal identical relative areas on each surface.

using isolation windows

Place a window on an area of your painting. Then position the other window in the identical area on the original art or photo. Compare the window that shows your painting to the window that shows the original photo or art. Because the isolation window forces you to "see" better, it becomes easy to determine if your area needs shape changes (to correct form), color changes (to correct hue), lightness or darkness changes (to correct value) or size changes (to correct proportion) in order to look more like the original. Remove the windows and compare the areas again with your "improved vision."

Use the windows to assist you in gradually changing and adjusting your painting to look like the original. With time, your eye will become trained to "isolate" areas and see them more accurately without using the windows.

On occasion, you will observe differences but prefer your own interpretation. This personal preference is encouraged. Isolation windows are for assisting you in improving your art, not for dictating choice.

Materials

Even though this is not a "project" book, you may find it helpful to know the materials I used when painting the nature art you find here and that I recommend for painting in general. Take a moment to compare your personal inventory with the items I mention below. You may want to add to your supplies accordingly.

Work Area

Although your work area is not an art material in itself, it is something that you should keep in mind when gathering your materials. You want a space that allows you to store your art supplies in a convenient and organized fashion.

Also keep in mind that highly detailed painting is best accomplished in a well-lit workspace with a light, neutral-colored work surface. A plain beige or gray, non-glare surface will not interfere with your perception of value and color. A hydraulic secretarial chair helps to position your body at the correct height over your work.

Painting Surfaces

Nature is an abundant source of subjects suitable for almost any surface or object. Canvas paintings, porcelain trinket boxes, walls, pillows, wooden plaques, furniture and metal trays are just a few possibilities. Smooth surfaces are optimum for detailed realistic portrayal.

Essential Aids

Gather resource photographs, a magnifying glass, color a[n] black-and-white enlargements of your subject, an acetate patte[rn] overlay and isolation windows, all of which are discussed [on] pages 10-11. These are essential aids for successful nature pain[t]ing.

Paints and Mediums

Select quality acrylic paints, which stay workable for lo[ng] periods of time and maintain clear, true color when mixe[d.] FolkArt Artists' Pigments, Jo Sonja's Artists' Colours, JansenA[rt] Traditions or quality tube acrylics, such as Liquitex Acryl[ic] Artist Color, provide optimum results when used with the tec[h]niques described in this book.

To further extend the open (working) time of your painti[ng] and to transparentize color glazes, choose FolkArt Blending G[el] Medium, Jo Sonja's Gel Retarder or Jo Sonja's Magic Mix. Th[e] gel mediums provide the greatest open time. Also, a layer of g[el] and paint may be removed long after it appears to [be] dry. Magic Mix may be used in place of a gel medium. It provid[es] less open time but enables smoother and more effortless blen[d]ing with a mop brush. Once dry, this medium creates a har[d,] non-removable layer of paint. Whether you use a gel medium [or] Magic Mix, keep it in a small cup separate from the wet palett[e.]

SILVER BRUSH LTD. BRUSHES USED TO PAINT THE ART IN THIS BOOK

BRUSH NAME	BRUSH SIZE(S)	BRUSH PURPOSE	BRUSH PHOTOGRAPH
Golden Natural shader	Nos. 2-10	For general painting	
Golden Natural filbert	Nos. 2-6	For general painting	
Ultra Mini angular	No. 12/0	Indispensable for tiny spaces	
Golden Natural round	Nos. 5/0 & 3/0	For exquisite detail	
Ultra Mini script liner	No. 20/0	For lining	
Ultra Mini designer round	No. 2	My favorite large liner	
Ruby Satin bright	Nos. 2 & 4	The best "eraser" for correcting	
Grand Prix white bristle round	No. 2	For creating texture	
Ruby Satin filbert grass comb	⅛-inch (3mm)	For fuzz and feathering	
Wee Mop	⅛-inch (3mm) to ½-inch (13mm)	For ease in blending	

Brushes

Only the highest-quality brushes in good condition are suitable for realistic painting. Each brush should be carefully selected not only for size and shape, but for compatibility of the fiber to the task to be performed. Also important is the pack, resilience and flexibility of the brush.

Soft-fiber flats are best for smooth undercoating and painting. Tiny rounds are essential for detail work. Resist the urge to use a liner for detailing. Liners are difficult to control unless being pulled to create a line. Liners should be strong at the ferrule and hold enough paint to complete the line with ease. Brights of extremely stiff fiber make the cleanest corrections. Professional white bristles create stippled textures. Stiff filbert grass combs, unopened and used with no pressure, give the best control when creating fuzz and feathered edges. An assortment of small, extremely soft hair mops is ideal for blending color into gels and mediums.

Miscellaneous Supplies

The following items will round out your painting supplies. Most are discussed in more detail in the next few pages.

- J.W. etc. UnderCover White Opaque Primer
- Ultra-fine grit sanding pad
- FolkArt Clearcote Acrylic Sealer (matte finish)
- J.W. etc.'s Right-Step Clear Varnish

- Mechanical pencil
- Tracing paper
- Saral transfer paper (white or gray)
- Stylus
- Kneaded eraser
- Water basin
- Small palette knife

- Masterson Sta-Wet Handy Palette
- Embossing dryer or hair dryer
- Denatured alcohol
- Rubber tipped lift-out tool
- Cotton swabs
- Soft paper towels

Preparation

The preparation stage is vital to setting the tone of your artistic experience. Taking time to prepare allows you to contemplate the events to come and predisposes you to focus. This is also the period of becoming better acquainted with your subject. Attention to detail, even at this early stage, can greatly influence the outcome of your art.

Preparing the Surface

The subjects in this book were painted on common poster board that was sprayed with matte acrylic sealer, base painted with acrylic paint and then resprayed before the design was applied.

Most surfaces should be sealed before applying a base paint. Both spray and brush-on sealers are available for use on specific surfaces. J.W. etc. UnderCover White Opaque Primer is a unique, all-purpose sealer that may be sanded to provide a super-smooth surface. It also has superior adherence to slick surfaces such as glass, metal and ceramic.

Once the surface is sealed, apply multiple coats of acrylic paint that has been thinned slightly with water. This results in smoother surfaces than one or two thick applications of paint.

Surface Preparation Supplies
FolkArt Clearcote Acrylic Sealer (matte), J. W. etc.'s Right-Step Clear Varnish (matte), J.W. etc. UnderCover White Opaque Primer, fine sanding pad.

The extra few minutes needed for additional thinned coats yield a more professional surface that is well worth the effort.

After the base paint is dry, check your work in outside light. Frequently, paint that appears to be opaque, smooth and free of streaks under your work lights will be flawed in the bright light of the out-of-doors. When imperfections appear in dry base paint, sand the surface with a fine sanding pad before applying subsequent layers of paint. Imperfections tend to be magnified with added coats of paint and are best removed as soon as possible.

Spray or lightly brush varnish the base color before transferring the pattern to the surface. The sealed surface allows effortless cleanup of smudges in the background and of stray paint along edges of shapes.

Tracing and Transferring

Tracing and transferring accurately is essential to the realistic representation of a subject. The smaller the subject, the less margin of error you have. Follow these tips for professional-quality tracing and transferring of designs:

- Use a mechanical pencil to trace your pattern.
- Trace the parts of the design which require the greatest accuracy first.
- Cut out the traced design to fit on the painting surface with no paper hanging over the edges of the surface. Excess paper hanging about the surface leads to slippage and errors. Position the tracing on the surface and tape it in two places.
- Select either white or gray transfer paper. Always remove excess graphite from the back of new graphite transfer paper with a soft paper towel. This will prevent overly dark pattern lines and graphite smudges in your base paint.
- Cut the transfer paper so it will not hang over the edges of the surface. Slip the transfer paper under the taped tracing-paper pattern.
- Use a fine-tipped stylus to transfer the design, transferring the most important elements first. Press lightly, as excess pressure on the stylus may dent the painting surface.

Tracing and Transferring Supplies
Transfer paper, tracing paper, stylus,
mechanical pencil, kneaded eraser.

Occasionally, it's easier to retrace a design with the mechanical pencil on the underneath side of your tracing paper rather than use transfer paper. To transfer the design, simply turn the paper over and retrace. This can work well for very tiny subjects or for positioning interior pattern lines on an undercoated subject.

Erase transfer lines with a kneaded eraser so lines are as pale as possible. Transfer lines can be difficult to remove or to cover later, even with opaque color.

Once a design is transferred, do not assume that it is perfect. The transferred pattern must be continually checked for accuracy as you paint..

Undercoating

If you're working on a colored surface (other than white or very light beige), undercoat the design in white before painting any colored undercoats. This will ensure an undercoat of purer color.

Sometimes it is advisable to undercoat an entire shape and then transfer interior design lines. Other times it is best to undercoat a subject in segments, leaving the original transfer lines exposed for awhile.

It is usually best to create an even, opaque undercoat. Even in acrylic paint, many colors are transparent to one degree or another and will not adequately cover a spotty or streaked undercoat.

When undercoating, use multiple coats of paint that have been thinned slightly with water. Apply the paint with a soft-fiber, flat brush of an appropriate size for the area. A round brush tends to leave valleys and ridges with each stroke. A 12/0 angular brush is excellent for undercoating small spaces. Some extremely small shapes or areas may need to be enhanced with a tiny round brush.

Studying the Subject

Before you begin the painting process, it is advisable to take a moment to compare the pattern to your resource art or photo and mentally note pattern line relationships to the finished piece. This brief interlude will help prevent possible misinterpretations later.

Entire Shape Undercoated

Segments Undercoated

Mixing Colors

The paints suggested for use in this book can be mixed to achieve an infinite variety of true color hues and values. Brush mixing automatically promotes the greatest range of color. Premix color only when large quantities of a consistent hue and value are needed.

Variety of hue and value may also be achieved with transparent layers of color. This process is called glazing. Value change occurs automatically when multiple transparent layers of the same hue and value are applied. Hue change occurs as the light filters through one transparent color to another and back to the eye. For example, placing a blue glaze over red will result in purple, blue over yellow results in green, and so on.

While a knowledge of color theory may enhance your ability to mix color, lack of it should not prevent you from experimenting. Trial and error can be a very effective teacher.

Basic Colors

All art for this book was created with the following FolkArt Artists' Pigments. For your convenience, conversions for JoSonja colors are listed in parentheses.

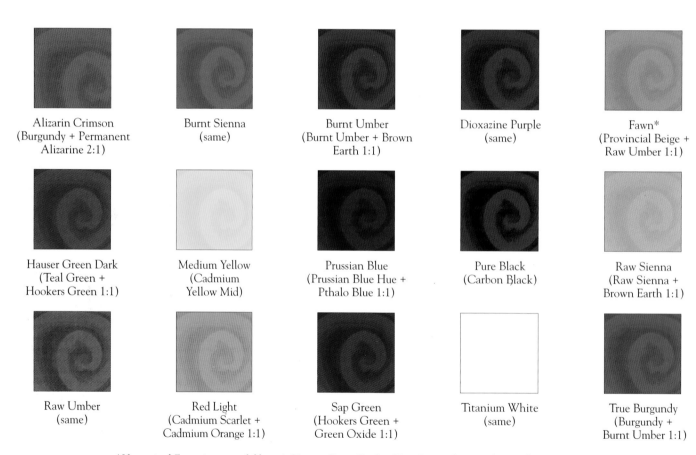

Alizarin Crimson (Burgundy + Permanent Alizarine 2:1)	Burnt Sienna (same)	Burnt Umber (Burnt Umber + Brown Earth 1:1)	Dioxazine Purple (same)	Fawn* (Provincial Beige + Raw Umber 1:1)
Hauser Green Dark (Teal Green + Hookers Green 1:1)	Medium Yellow (Cadmium Yellow Mid)	Prussian Blue (Prussian Blue Hue + Pthalo Blue 1:1)	Pure Black (Carbon Black)	Raw Sienna (Raw Sienna + Brown Earth 1:1)
Raw Umber (same)	Red Light (Cadmium Scarlet + Cadmium Orange 1:1)	Sap Green (Hookers Green + Green Oxide 1:1)	Titanium White (same)	True Burgundy (Burgundy + Burnt Umber 1:1)

If premixed Fawn is not available, mix Hauser Green Dark + True Burgundy + Medium Yellow (1:1:5).

Color Mixes

A grid of color-mix swatches, like the example at the lower right of the opposite page, is located on the lower right of each subject section in this book. These represent a sampling, but not all, of the color mixes used in the art seen on those pages and are intended only to be used as a starting point for color selection and mixing.

These mixes are identified by number and may be referenced on the next page for the specific color combinations needed to recreate each mix. These color combinations are not specific formulas but a list of the component colors of each swatch. Swatches that appear to be very different may have the same color mix chart number because they were mixed with identical

...mponent colors but in different proportions. In the illustration ...the right, you can see a range of colors possible with color mix ...(Sap Green + Raw Umber + Medium Yellow + Titanium ...'hite) from the list below.

Component colors are listed in no particular order. Before ...ixing, determine on which side of the value scale (from black ...white) the color falls. If the mix falls on the light half of the ...ale, begin mixing with the lightest colors in the mix. If it falls ...the darker half, begin with the darkest colors in the mix. This ...events inadvertently mixing more color than is needed as you ...ljust the value and hue. Add component colors gradually, con- ...antly checking results as you mix.

Determining the true color of a mix on the palette may ...difficult. Before painting, check the hue and value of a mix by ...illing a streak of transparent color away from the puddle. Also,

Color Range

Seen here are just a few examples of colors that may be mixed from color mix 6 (Sap Green + Raw Umber + Medium Yellow + Titanium White). By varying the proportion of the component colors, you may change the value, intensity and hue of the mix.

because artificial light affects color perception, it's best to look at mixes in bright daylight. Use your eye and feel free to individualize your mixes, as there is seldom a need for an exact match to the original subject.

COLOR MIX COMPONENTS

Fawn
Burnt Umber + Fawn
Dioxazine Purple + Raw Sienna
Sap Green + Raw Umber
Sap Green + Raw Umber
+ Medium Yellow
Sap Green + Raw Umber + Medium
Yellow + Titanium White
Sap Green + Prussian Blue
Sap Green + Prussian Blue
+ Titaniun White
Burnt Umber + Burnt Sienna
). Burnt Sienna + Medium Yellow
. Sap Green + Medium Yellow
. Sap Green + Pure Black
. Sap Green + Titaniun White
. Medium Yellow + Burnt Sienna
+ Red Light
. Medium Yellow + Titanium White
+ Sap Green
. Prussian Blue + Titanium White
+ Pure Black
. Prussian Blue + Dioxazine Purple
+ Titanium White
. Medium Yellow + Titanium White
. Fawn + Titanium White
+ Medium Yellow

20. Raw Umber + Titanium White
+ Pure Black
21. Medium Yellow + Red Light
22. Fawn + Titanium White + Sap Green
23. Raw Sienna + Medium Yellow
24. Raw Sienna + Red Light
25. Dioxazine Purple + Titanium White
26. Dioxazine Purple + Alizarin Crimson
27. Alizarin Crimson + Titanium White
28. Red Light + Titanium White
29. Alizarin Crimson + Red Light
30. Alizarin Crimson + Burnt Sienna
31. Burnt Sienna + Fawn
32. Raw Umber + Medium Yellow
33. Alizarin Crimson + Dioxazine Purple
+ Titanium White
34. Medium Yellow + Sap Green
+ Alizarin Crimson
35. Fawn + Titanium White
36. Fawn + Pure Black +
Titanium White
37. Sap Green + Titanium White
+ Pure Black
38. Alizarin Crimson + Burnt Sienna
+ Titanium White
39. Raw Umber + Titanium White
40. Alizarin Crimson + True Burgundy

This is a sample color mix grid that you'll find at the lower right of almost every subject section. The numbers correspond to the color mix component list on this page. Note that the same components may result in different colors, depending on the proportions used.

Painting Techniques

It is important to remember that there is no right or wrong in art—only cause and effect. If your action has caused a less-than-optimum effect, the techniques described here allow for infinite changing of your work. Relax, for nothing you paint need be forever. You have infinite opportunities to change and improve your painting.

The gel mediums introduced into the acrylic industry in recent years make possible traditional blending and glazing techniques once used only with oil colors. It's now possible to control the transparency and open time of the paint, depending on the amount of gel used. The gels facilitate beautiful, smooth transitions from one color into another. Color may also be blended into adjacent transparent gel. The color will become transparent to the point of nothingness, letting the previous layer of paint show through. Gel also is especially valuable for creating brilliant highlights and sparkling reflections. (See "Paints and Mediums," page 12, for additional information about gels and Magic Mix medium.)

Blending

For ease in blending, moisten an area with gel before painting. While the paint is wet, blend the paint by gently whisking a small mop about the area until brush marks are no longer visible and a smooth transition is achieved. Use no pressure whatsoever. Frequently wipe excess paint from the mop. Control color distribution with the direction you whisk the mop.

Embossing Dryer

This tool, which looks like a tiny hair dryer of about 7" (18cm) long, allows you to dry paints and mediums quickly. The embossing dryer is quiet and does not blow air around. You can also use an actual hair dryer.

Layering

Multiple layers of gel and paint may be used to perfect a painting. Usually the transparent nature of the paint as it combines with the gel will require more than one application to achieve desired effect. It's extremely important to make sure the previous layer of gel and paint is dry before proceeding. The paints recommended in this book may feel dry to the touch, but may lift upon contact with more paint, water, or gel. Force drying with high heat is an integral part of the process. Always allow the surface to cool before continuing.

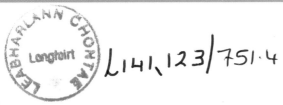

L141,123/751.4

ealing

ealing a layer of dry gel and paint with matte acrylic spray (or
light coat of varnish) may be done at any time and enables you
 continue painting and perfecting your work with no fear of
amaging an underlying layer. Sealing also serves to reveal the
ue color of the dried paint, and the slick surface aids in paint-
g extremely fine detail. Both these qualities are beneficial for
alistic portrayal.

Glazing

lazing simply means painting a layer of transparent color over
 existing dry layer of color, thereby automatically changing
e hue or value of the underlying color. For large areas, gel may
 premixed with color to make it transparent and then painted
ver existing dry paint. For smaller areas, it is preferable to apply
 slick of gel to the surface before the paint. The paint will
come a transparent glaze as it mixes with the gel when blend-
 with a mop. (See page 16 for further discussion of glazes.)

Glazing has several attributes that make it especially well-
ited for realistic painting:

Glazing creates glowing, luminous color that is difficult to
achieve with other techniques. It is usually preferable to glaze
darker-value color over light-value colors. Light color glazes
over dark color often result in a hazy or milky glaze.

A glaze of white or base paint color, can be used to make specific design elements recede into the background.

While still wet, glazes may be manipulated with brushes or
lift-out tools to create the illusion of texture or razor-sharp
lines such as leaf veins.

Most important, glazes allow you to gradually layer the complicated maze of patterns, shading and reflections which
occur in nature.

Detailing

ealistic nature painting demands detail. Creating exquisite
etail work is extremely dependent on controlling the consis-
ncy of your paint and the pressure on your brush. While a wet
alette, such as Sta-Wet palettes by Masterson, keeps paint
oist, paint rarely, if ever, should be used without thinning with
ater to one degree or another so that it flows effortlessly and
onsistently from the brush. Constantly be aware of your pres-

Lift-Out Tool
A lift-out tool is useful to create bumpy textures found in nature.

**Masterson's
Sta-Wet Palette**

**Varnishes
for Finishing**

sure levels on your brush to help control the line or shape you
are creating.

Finishing
Acrylic paint must be varnished in some manner to bring out the
true color and beauty of the painting. Even matte varnish will
greatly enhance your work.

Perfecting Your Work

I FREQUENTLY TELL STUDENTS, "IT'S NOT WHAT YOU DO, BUT WHAT YOU DO ABOUT IT!" ESTABLISH THE HABIT OF CONSTANTLY ASKING YOURSELF IF THIS IS THE BEST YOU CAN DO.

The techniques in this book allow for endless perfecting. If your work is less than your best, change it. Raising the standard of work you will accept from yourself, the simple act of asking for better, often results in dramatic improvement in your work.

Continually scrutinize your work at each stage of development. Less than your best effort early in the painting only makes subsequent stages more difficult to perfect. In the process of perfecting, you will learn much about how well you are seeing your subject. Correcting and perfecting existing work escalates your ability to see a subject more accurately, while starting over often results only in repeating the same errors. Our brains are essentially lazy, so once the brain has been forced to make corrections and improvements, it will prefer in the future to avoid the experience and guide the hand more attentively in the first place.

Refrain from evaluating your entire painting at once. Instead, concentrate on one small area at a time. This prevents becoming lost and frustrated, unable to determine what to do next. Learn to think in terms of making each small area "prettier," rather than "perfect." As you repeatedly make each small area "prettier," the overall quality of your painting will spiral upward.

If an area is less than satisfactory, employ your isolation windows to find the subtle differences in your painting from the original photograph or art. Then perfect the area until it more closely matches the original.

Often your work needs nothing more than continuing to overpaint detail upon detail, glaze upon glaze. I find that students are inclined to give up too soon. All that is really needed for a spectacular painting is perseverance!

Check your work with a magnifying glass. You will be amazed to see imperfections which you, in fact, were able to see with the naked eye, but had accepted as satisfactory. Once these imperfections are greatly enlarged, they become intolerable and demand further attention.

Sometimes, removal of paint is necessary to perfect the work. To remove unwanted paint, first try lifting off the paint with water. If that fails, denatured alcohol will probably suffice. A stiff bright brush or a cotton swab dipped in water or alcohol and then blotted on a paper towel are excellent clean-up tools. Paper towels used by themselves to remove paint from a background tend to smear rather than lift the paint.

Keep in mind that only clean lift-out tools will pristinely remove unwanted color. The wet bright brush must be wiped clean after each stroke. The swab must be rotated to a clean side or replaced with a clean swab with each stroke. To continue scrubbing an area with a dirty tool only creates a smear, or even worse, grinds the offending paint into the surface. Remove unwanted paint slowly, allowing the water or alcohol to float the color to the surface before being gently removed.

Once paint has cured or been sprayed with sealer, you will most certainly need to gently scrape it off with an X-acto blade, a precision tool for removing unwanted paint. It is especially effective for sharpening the edges of shapes. Scrape the paint gently with the blade positioned at a low angle to the surface. For best results, the blade must be razor-sharp at all times. Keep a good stock handy and change your blade frequently.

Smudges or blurry edges extending into the background are best removed rather than overpainted, since old color tends to ghost through new paint once the paint has cured. After the unwanted color has been removed, it may be necessary to repaint an area of base paint which has been rubbed or scraped thin. Smudges should be removed immediately. Not only will this prevent permanent stains, it will also serve to keep you in a perfection mode mentally.

ONCE YOU MAKE IT A HABIT NEVER TO SETTLE FOR LESS THAN YOUR BEST PAINTING, YOU WILL ALWAYS BE ABLE TO FIND A WAY TO ACHIEVE IT.

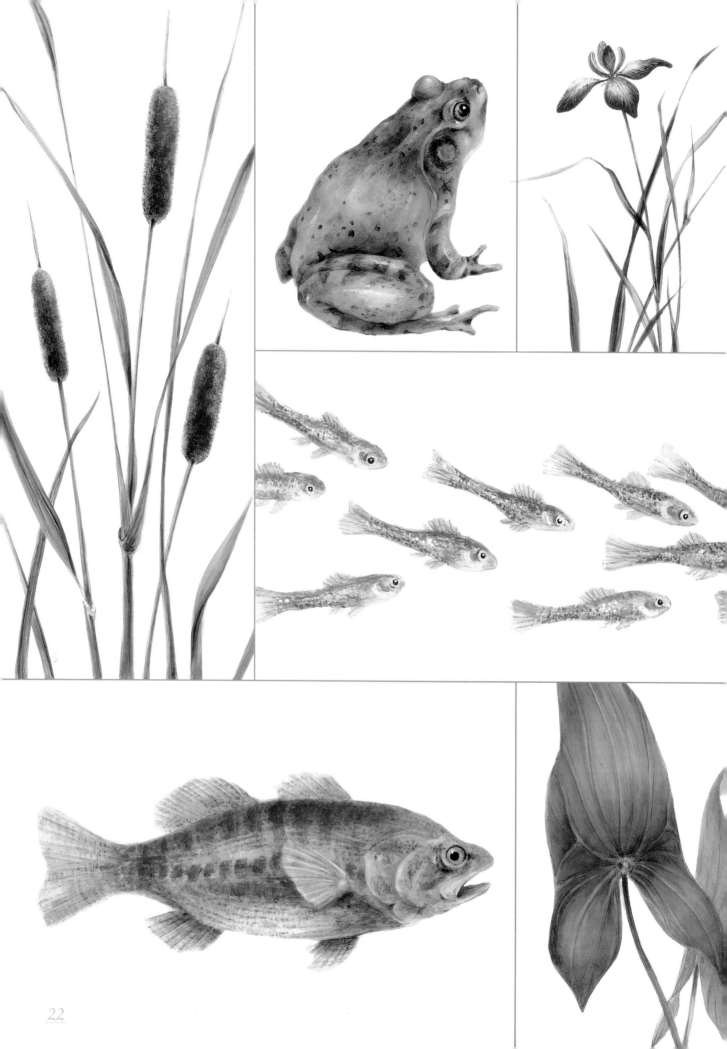

Ponds & Streams

Water is the driving
force of all nature.

—Leonardo Da Vinci

Fish & Water Life

REALISTIC DEPICTION OF FISH IS MOST EASILY ACCOMPLISHED WITH OVERLAYS OF TRANS
PARENT COLOR TO ESTABLISH COMPLICATED PATTERNS AND REFLECTIONS. CONSIDERABL
ARTISTIC LICENSE IS POSSIBLE BECAUSE ENDLESS VARIATION OCCURS WITHIN A SPECIES.

1
UNDERCOAT
with blues and yellow.

2
ESTABLISH
the scale pattern methodically.

Minnows are so small, they may be mistaken for baby fish.

Clear delineation of the head adds realism to fish.

3
SHADE
and highlight with glazes.

4
CONTINUE
to glaze and add details.

Iridescent scales reflect light in all the colors of the rainbow.

Eye color is important when identifying species.

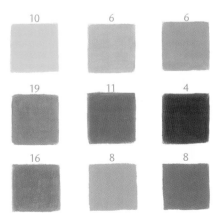

10	6	6
19	11	4
16	8	8

Color mix reference chart is on page 17.

PONDS AND STREAMS ARE NOT INHABITED ONLY BY FISH. A BACKWARD-SWIMMING CRAWDAD MAKES A COMICAL ADDITION TO WATER SCENES. TINY TADPOLES EVOKE MEMORIES OF OUR CHILDHOOD FASCINATION WITH THE MIRACULOUS CYCLE OF LIFE.

1
BASE
the body segments with a bright yellow-orange.

2
SHADE
the body segments with dark brown.
Blend with a tiny mop brush.

Newly hatched tadpoles are velvety black.

The tiny legs form and emerge knees first.

Any size catfish is plausible to paint, since they never cease growing.

3
GLAZE
egments with a slick of gel medium and transparent red color.

4
PERFECT
shading with multiple color glazes to create
a luminous hard shell. Add distinctive details.

A tadpole may be either a frog or a toad.

Tail remnants linger on the infant amphibian.

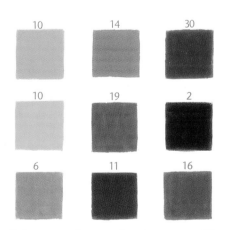

Two dorsal fins are either distinctly separate or merge as one.

Color mix reference chart is on page 17.

Dragonflies & Damselflies

DRAGONFLIES AND DAMSELFLIES ARE BENEFICIAL INSECTS. HATCHED IN PONDS AND STREAMS, THESE IRIDESCENT CREATURES ARE MOST OFTEN FOUND NEAR WATER. SCIENTISTS HAVE DISCOVERED FOSSIL REMAINS OF DRAGONFLIES WITH 38" (97CM) WINGSPANS.

1
UNDERCOAT
the head with yellow-green and the body with fawn and black. Moisten the wings with gel medium and blend in transparent blue-green.

2
SHADE
the head with darker green and the body with dark brown. Intensify the wing color.

Dragonflies are large insects with a wingspan up to 6" (15cm). The wings are at right angles to the body at all times.

Some dragonflies are chubby and have patterned wings.

Eyes large and close

Eyes smaller and on sides

Dragonfly eyes are large and usually meet in the middle of the head. The compound eyes provide 360° vision with only a small blind spot to the rear, making it easiest to approach the insect from behind.

Damselfly eyes are smaller and are placed on the sides of the head. Eyes that are far apart help the insect accurately judge distance. Dragonflies and damselflies hunt during the day, ridding the environment of pesky flies and mosquitoes.

3
HIGHLIGHT
the head with white and yellow. Create the
turquoise and yellow markings. Establish the dominant
vein patterns with dark brown.

4
INDICATE
inferior vein structure. Continue to perfect the
coloration and reflections with glazes.

Damselflies are smaller, more slender and delicate, with wings
that fold over the body when at rest.

Both have extremely short antennae.

11	1	2
11	7	16
12	26	25

Both dragonflies and damselflies span the spectrum of colors.

Color mix reference chart is on page 17.

Water Lilies & Arrowheads

MODERN WATER LILIES ARE A FORM OF THE PREHISTORIC LOTUS PLANT. THE ARROWHEAD IS ANOTHER ANCIENT WATER PLANT WITH ATTRACTIVE FLOWERS. THE DISTINCTLY ROUND OR TRIANGULAR SHAPES OF BOTH PLANTS ARE COMPOSITIONAL PERFECTION.

1
UNDERCOAT
and shade individual petals and the center.

Arrowhead plants may be narrow, rounded, . . .

2
DEFINE
layers of petals with deeper color glazes.

3
HIGHLIGHT
and further define the separate petals. Undercoat, shade
and highlight the floating pads with multiple values of green.

. . . fat or even grasslike in their structure.

Color mix reference chart is on page 17.

Frogs

FROGS COME IN A VAST ARRAY OF SIZES, SHAPES AND COLORATIONS. SHADE AND HIGHLIGHT FOR FORM BEFORE ADDING SKIN PATTERNS. EYE PUPILS VARY FROM VERTICAL SLITS TO ROUND TO HORIZONTAL. MOST TRUE FROGS ARE SMOOTH-SKINNED, WEB-TOED AND LONG-LEGGED FOR LEAPING

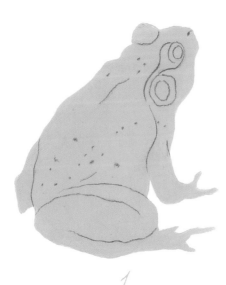

1
UNDERCOAT
with pale yellow-green. Transfer the interior pattern.

2
ESTABLISH
the ear disc and eye undercoats. Moisten with gel medium and blend in pale highlights and darker green shading.

Tree frogs may live anywhere, not just in trees.

Ultra-smooth skin and large eyes are typical.

Frogs can have elaborate patterns and coloration.

Some adult frogs may be as small as ⅝" (16mm).

3
ENHANCE
highlights and shading.
Add color glazes of fawn and dark green.

4
CONTINUE
to layer glazes of gel medium and color. Paint speckles and
leg patterns with transparent dark brown. Perfect the details.

Most North American tree frogs are green or brown.

Sticky toe discs are cute and aid in climbing.

Not all frogs are green (and not all toads are brown).

Color mix reference chart is on page 17.

Cattails & Blue Flags

CATTAIL AND BLUE FLAG STANDS ARE FOUND IN OR NEAR WATER. CATTAIL LEAVES ARE ALWAYS TALLER THAN THE FLOWER STALKS. BLUE FLAG IS A WILD IRIS. IT'S A SOURCE OF DYE AND OF THE ORRIS ROOT USED IN FOLK MEDICINE.

1

UNDERCOAT
with a light yellow-brown, preserving
the strict parallel edges.

Undercoat, shade and highlight with different
values of green. Maintain razor-sharp edges.

2
APPLY
gel medium and gently tap in rust-colored texture with a bristle brush.

3
ADD
deep brown velvety texture while the paint is still wet. Use a tiny mop brush, applying no pressure.

4
PERFECT
edge fuzz with a filbert grass comb. Then finish with color glazes.

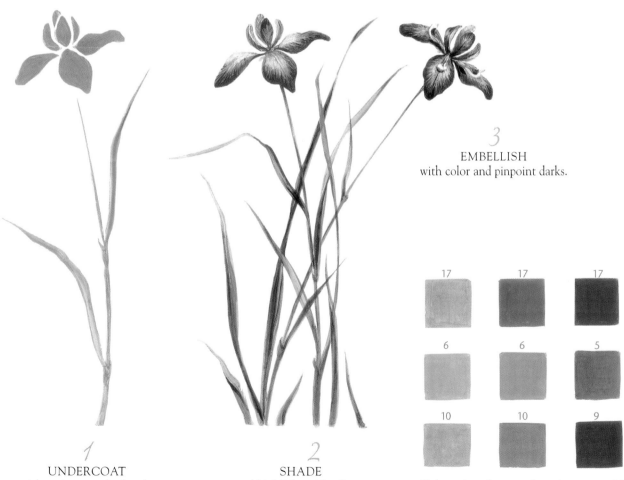

3
EMBELLISH
with color and pinpoint darks.

1
UNDERCOAT
with a tiny angular brush.

2
SHADE
and highlight with a liner.

Color mix reference chart is on page 17.

Turtles

MULTIPLE GLAZES WITH GEL MEDIUM ALLOW THE ARTIST TO MORE EASILY PORTRAY REAL-ISTIC INTRICATE SHELL PATTERNS OF TURTLES. MOST WATER TURTLES HAVE MORE ELABO-RATE BODY PATTERNS AND FLATTER SHELLS THAN LAND TURTLES.

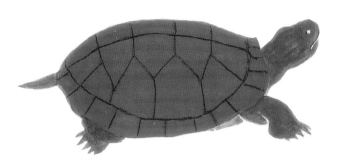

1
UNDERCOAT
the shell with neutral brown and the body
with olive green. Transfer the shell pattern.

2
CREATE
the rudimentary shell and body patterns with a tiny
round brush and light yellow and bright red.

While all turtles seem to have grouchy, turned-down mouths,
snapping turtles are as mean as they look! Like all turtles, snappers have
no teeth. They are the only turtles with sawback tails.

Turtles have no vocal chords but can hiss.

Soft-shelled turtles look like floating pancakes.

3
APPLY
gel medium and stroke in shell ridges with a
filbert grass comb. Embellish colored markings.

4
APPLY
multiple color glazes, drying between layers, to create
the translucent shell. Perfect all markings.

Baby turtles are cutely awkward with large heads, tiny tails,
stubby limbs and disproportionately small shells. Adult turtle size varies
greatly, since turtles continue to grow their entire lives.

A few turtle species have sawback shells.

Color mix reference chart is on page 17.

Meadows & Hills

Nature will bear the closest inspection.
She invites us to lay our eye level
with her smallest leaf and take
an insect view of its plain.

—Henry David Thoreau

Grasses & Foxtails

GRASSES ARE MUCH MORE THAN SIMPLISTIC GREEN BLADES. THEY HAVE SHAPE AND FORM AND SHOULD BE TREATED AS COMPOSITIONS UNTO THEMSELVES—NEVER AS AN AFTER-THOUGHT IN A PAINTING. USE A VARIETY OF COLOR VALUES ON EACH AND EVERY BLADE.

1
UNDERCOAT
with a light green and stipple darker green with a tiny mop.

Many grasses grow from a single point.

Some grasses are flowing . . .

. . . while others are spiky . .

2
ADD
fine, long, darker green strokes with a liner.

3
GLAZE
with gel medium and white. Continue
to add details, layer by layer.

Diverse seed heads add interest.

Flower heads may appear with the seasons.

. . . or even woody in structure.

Color mix reference chart is on page 17.

Clover

CLOVER FLOWERS HAVE VERY INTRICATE PETALS. THE PLANT MAY HAVE A GROWTH PATTERN OF A SINGLE STEM OR SEVERAL STEMS IN A CLUMP. THE LEAVES ARE SOFT AND SLIGHTLY FUZZED, AND THEY ALWAYS DISPLAY A DISTINCTIVE WHITISH "V" PATTERN.

1
UNDERCOAT
the flower with pink and the leaves with medium green.

2
SHADE
the leaves and establish petal depth with darker value greens.

Under magnification, clover petals are like tiny flowers unto themselves.

Rabbit foot clover has unusual fuzzy flower heads.

Field clovers appear in a wide range of colors.

3
HIGHLIGHT
the leaves. Then create a radiating petal pattern with white.

4
PERFECT
with ultra-fine liner strokes and a succession of color glazes.

Common white clover must be painted with more dark values than white.

Leaf shapes may vary, but all varieties have three leaflets.

Color mix reference chart is on page 17.

Grasshoppers & Others

GRASSHOPPERS, LOCUSTS, CICADAS AND KATYDIDS ARE ALL MEMBERS OF THE NOISY GRASSHOPPER FAMILY. LOCUSTS ARE SHORTHORN GRASSHOPPERS THAT HAVE CHANGED COLOR AND GATHER IN SWARMS. GRASSHOPPERS HAVE AN EXTRA SET OF EYES AT THE TIPS OF THEIR ANTENNAE.

1
UNDERCOAT
the body segments with pale green.

2
ESTABLISH
the black eye. Moisten with gel medium and blend in darker green shading.

Nymphs have large heads and eyes in proportion to their bodies.

Minute leaf hoppers provide a variety of splendid designs and colors.

The praying mantis reserves its front legs for catching prey.

Cicadas have extremely short antennae. They appear in cycle of years, the cycle length varying according to cicada type.

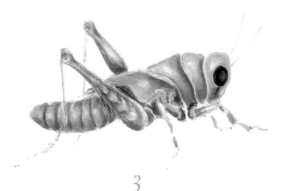

3
DEVELOP
the form with blended white highlights.

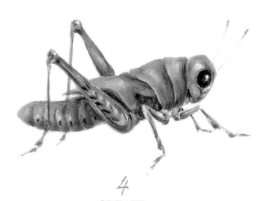

4
CREATE
brown air holes along the abdomen. Perfect the coloration and reflections with glazes.

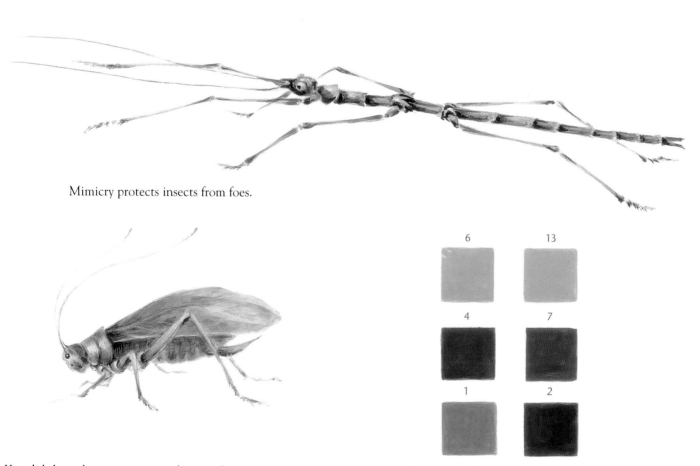

Mimicry protects insects from foes.

Katydids have long antennae and wings that mimic leaves.

Color mix reference chart is on page 17.

Vines

VINES HAVE ADAPTED TO THEIR ENVIRONMENT BY ELONGATING. SOME SCRAMBLE ALONG THE GROUND; OTHERS CLIMB WITH ROOTS AND PADS; MANY SIMPLY CLING—ATTACHING WITH TENDRILS, CATCHING WITH THORNS OR TWINING ON OTHER PLANTS.

1
UNDERCOAT
leaves with medium green and stems
with light brown.

2
APPLY
a slick of gel medium and blend in
shading with a tiny mop brush.

Many wild vines are ancestors of some
of our most common garden plants.

Vines have infinite combinations of
leaf types and growth patterns, . . .

3
BLEND
in lighter green highlights. Then
add the details, layer by layer.

19	27	15
6	25	11
4	8	7

. . . some to the point of defying even an artist's imagination.

Color mix reference chart is on page 17.

Vines, continued

VINES ARE FREQUENTLY RAMPANT AND EVEN INVASIVE GROWERS. STEMS MAY BE WOODY OR FIBROUS. FRUIT AND FLOWERS ON VINES ARE AN EASILY ACCESSIBLE SOURCE OF FOOD FOR INSECTS AND BIRDS.

1
ESTABLISH
pink and yellow undercoats
with a flat brush.

2
APPLY
a slick of gel medium and blend
in deeper shading.

1
UNDERCOAT
leaves and stem with
light greens and browns.

2
SHADE
with darker values of
green and brown.

3

BLEND
in highlights. Then add glazes and
details, one layer at a time.

4

PERFECT
with glazes and add delicate
details with a liner.

3

HIGHLIGHT
the shapes with lighter
values of color.

When painting very
light-value flowers, keep in
mind that the true color of
the flower will be evident
only in a few places as light
and shadow play over the
flower and define its form.

18	21	28
15	2	29
6	11	8

Color mix reference chart is on page 17.

Raspberries & Strawberries

WILD RASPBERRIES AND STRAWBERRIES ARE RELATED TO ROSES, BUT ONLY RASPBERRIES HAVE THORNS. THE STRAWBERRY IS ARTISTICALLY INTERESTING IN THAT IT BEARS FLOWERS AND FRUIT SIMULTANEOUSLY. BOTH HAVE COMPOUND LEAVES OF THREE LEAFLETS.

1

UNDERCOAT
and shade the leaves with two values of green. Establish the forms of the berries.

1

UNDERCOAT
with red-orange.

1

BASE
the leaves with medium and dark green.

2
APPLY
...el medium and highlight the leaves with lighter values of green. Shade the berries.

3
ENHANCE
with glazes and add details.

2
SHADE
with darker-value red.

3
HIGHLIGHT
with pale yellow.

2
EMBELLISH
with lighter values of green.

Color mix reference chart is on page 17.

Queen Anne's Lace

QUEEN ANNE'S LACE, A SOMEWHAT SCRAGGLY WILDFLOWER WHEN VIEWED INDIVIDUALL
IS BREATHTAKING WHEN SEEN EN MASSE IN SUMMER FIELDS. THOUGH A SINGLE PLANT
ISN'T OFTEN DEPICTED, ITS INTRICATE STRUCTURE IS IMPORTANT TO UNDERSTAND .

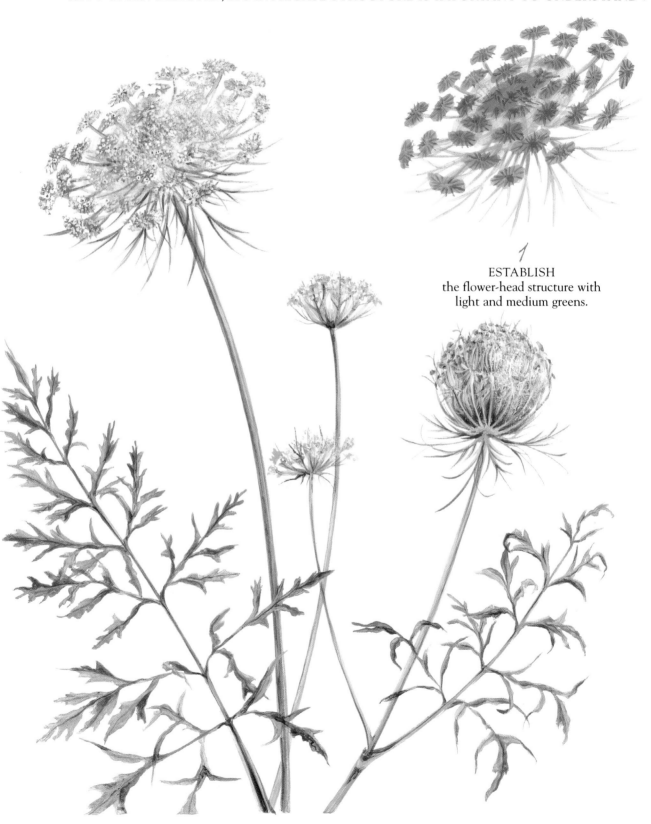

1
ESTABLISH
the flower-head structure with
light and medium greens.

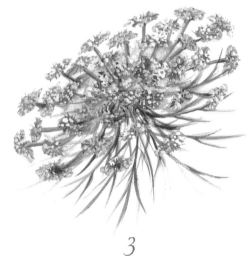

2
INDICATE
miniature florets with gel medium and dots of white.

3
SHADE
and then continue to embellish the flower with glazes.

1
PAINT
the basic form of the unopened flower.

2
SHADE,
perfect details and add color glazes.

Block in the leaf shape with mid-value green.
Proceed to shade, highlight and add minimal vein details.

6	19
6	27
6	27

Color mix reference chart is on page 17.

ALL INSECTS POSSESS THREE BASIC BODY PARTS—A HEAD, A THORAX (WHERE WINGS AN[
LEGS ATTACH) AND AN ABDOMEN. BEYOND THAT, THE VARIETY IS SO VAST AS TO BOGGL[
EVEN THE WILDEST IMAGINATION.

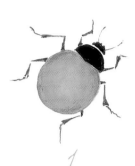   

1

UNDERCOAT
brightly with yellow
and orange.

2

ENHANCE
the form with deep red.

3

ESTABLISH
specifics with the pattern
and leg details.

4

ADD
life with shining highlights

Insect legs may appear to extend
from the wing cases, but are attached
to the thorax underneath.

While it is beneficial to know
insect particulars, . . .

. . . it is often more realistic
to paint only the essence.

    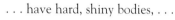

Ants come in red, black or brown, . . .

. . . have hard, shiny bodies, . . .

An insect's skeleton can be on the outside.

Often antennae are segmented. Patterns are simple to comple[

We usually think of ladybugs as red . . .

. . . but some are green or orange.

Ladybugs have short antennae.

Patterns range from many to few spots.

Many beetles have hard wing cases, . . .

. . . which lift to reveal their true flight wings.

. . . can be large or almost minuscule . . .

. . . and have a pronounced waist.

Razor-sharp edges and bright reflections connote hard shells.

Color mix reference chart is on page 17.

Butterflies

ALTHOUGH WE TEND NOT THINK OF THEM AS SUCH, BUTTERFLIES ARE INSECTS AND HAVE THE ATTRIBUTES OF INSECTS, NAMELY, SIX LEGS AND A THREE-PART BODY (HEAD, THORAX AND ABDOMEN). BUTTERFLIES HAVE TWO FOREWINGS AND TWO HIND WINGS.

1
UNDERCOAT
with pale greenish yellow.
Transfer the vein pattern.

2
ADD
the eyes and antennae. Moisten with gel medium
and blend in darker shading.

Top wings overlap bottom wings
when seen from above.

Bottom wings overlap top wings
when seen from below.

Butterflies have long tongues and smooth
antennae with knobs at the tips.

Observe differing wing shapes, . . .

. . . body sizes and shapes . . .

3

PAINT
delicate vein lines with a liner and white.
Remove the transfer lines.

4

PERFECT
with a series of white and color glazes.
Add details and pinpoint darks.

The top sides of wings often have a
brilliantly marked pattern.

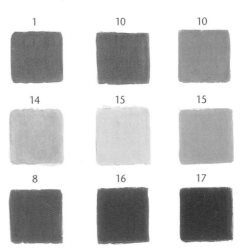

The undersides of wings are different in appearance
from the top sides and are frequently plainer.

1	10	10
14	15	15
8	16	17

. . . and markings of similar butterflies.

Color mix reference chart is on page 17.

Butterflies, continued

WHILE IT IS HELPFUL TO STUDY STATIC BUTTERFLIES FROM A DIRECT OVERHEAD VIEW, IT IS USUALLY MORE NATURAL AND LIFELIKE TO DEPICT THEM IN VARIOUS OTHER POSITION OF REST AND FLIGHT. MAKE YOUR BUTTERFLIES FLUTTER!

1
UNDERCOAT
with golden orange and light brown.
Transfer the vein pattern.

2
SHADE
the wings with deeper color. Establish the eyes,
and the dark body, vein and wing patterns.

Observe butterfly wing and body positions . . .

. . . while at rest, . . .

Some varieties' wings are angular rather than rounded in shape.

Portray resting butterflies with wings above the back.

3
ADD
light colors and highlights
on the wings and body.

4
ENHANCE
with glazes of light and dark colors.
Perfect the details with a liner.

. . . as seen from below . . .

. . . and from varying overhead angles.

Butterfly bodies are velvety and may be intricately patterned.

Color mix reference chart is on page 17.

Dandelions

THROUGHOUT HISTORY EURASIAN DANDELIONS HAVE BEEN ENCOURAGED TO GROW AN
HAVE EVEN BEEN IMPORTED AROUND THE WORLD. FOR MANY THEY'VE BEEN A SOURCE OF
FOOD AND MEDICINE. FOR CHILDREN THEY'RE A CONTINUING SOURCE OF SIMPLE DELIGH

1

UNDERCOAT
the disc with bright yellow. Mark the center
and establish the ellipse.

1

UNDERCOAT
precisely the jagged arrowhead leaves.

1

COAT
the area with gel. Gradually stipple in misty color with a mo

2
APPLY
a slick of gel. Load a designer round brush with thinned brown tipped in yellow. Stroke radiating petals from the rim toward the center.

3
LOAD
the brush with thinned tan tipped with yellow, and continue to stroke in petals to the center. Emphasize highlights and perfect the details.

2
SHADE
the leaf and turned edges with deep green.

3
HIGHLIGHT
the form. Then paint the veins with a liner.

2
POSITION
the seeds.

3
CREATE
tiny parachutes of fluff for each seed.

Color mix reference chart is on page 17.

Bees

BUMBLE BEES AND HONEY BEES ARE PERHAPS THE MOST COMMONLY PAINTED INSECTS. WHILE IT ISN'T NECESSARY OR EVEN DESIRABLE TO BE ANATOMICALLY PRECISE IN EVERY PAINTING, CAREFUL OBSERVATION WILL HELP YOU PAINT MORE LIFELIKE BEES.

1

BASE
the bee with yellow and black.
Accurately segment the legs with light brown.

2

APPLY
gel medium and blend in darker values with a filbert grass comb. Darken the legs.

Queen bees are outsized and have long abdomens for holding eggs. The queen is seldom seen outside the hive.

Worker bees are sterile females. These are the bees seen on flowers, often with legs laden with golden pollen.

Hovering bees have dangling legs.

In flight, bee legs may seem to flail about.

3
HIGHLIGHT
the body and establish a hint of wing veining
with gel medium and color.

4
EMBELLISH
the fuzz with a script liner. Complete the
highlighting with touches of white.

Drones are males and have large eyes to locate a queen
for mating. They do not work and are not seen on flowers.

A bee leg is much like any other insect leg. Its five major joints must
bend in correct positions for the insect to look realistic. Legs aren't as
fun to paint as stripes and wings, but they require equal attention.

el mediums are indispensable for depicting transparent wings.

Color mix reference chart is on page 17.

Black-Eyed Susans

BLACK-EYED SUSANS ARE PROLIFIC WILDFLOWERS OF THE EXTENSIVE SUNFLOWER FAMILY. FLOWER HEADS MAY HAVE EIGHT TO TWENTY-SOME DROOPING YELLOW PETALS AROUND SPIRALED BROWN CENTER. LEAVES AND STEMS ARE CHARACTERISTICALLY HAIRY.

1

UNDERCOAT
with bright yellow, green and light tan.

1

ESTABLISH
the curves of the seed spirals.

1

BASE AND SHADE
with two values of green. Stroke in the dominant vein patter

2
BLEND
in shading with gel medium and a mop.

3
HIGHLIGHT
and then continue to glaze color and add detail.

2
FILL IN
spirals of dark spots methodically.

3
SHADE
with complementary deep purple.

2
INDICATE
secondary veins. Then highlight and add brown glazes.

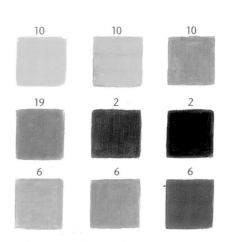

Color mix reference chart is on page 17.

Moths

MOTHS ARE FATTER AND HAIRIER THAN BUTTERFLIES BECAUSE MANY ARE NOCTURNAL WITH NO SUN TO WARM THEM AT NIGHT. THEIR SCALY WINGS ARE DELICATELY FUZZED. MOTHS, WHILE PESKY, CAN BE AS BEAUTIFUL AND COLORFUL AS BUTTERFLIES.

1
UNDERCOAT
with deep peach and beige.
Transfer the interior pattern.

2
PRECISELY PAINT
the black wing and body patterns. Notice how much lighter colors appear when black is placed next to them.

"Eyes" and other patterns help dissuade predators.

Moth antennae are fuzzy and mimic tiny ferns.

1
UNDERCOAT
and shade the segmented caterpillar body.

2
HIGHLIGHT
the segments with light green and white.

3
MOISTEN
with gel medium. Shade the forewings with
deeper color and highlight the hind wings with white.
Fuzz the body, head and antennae with a liner.

4
PERFECT
with a series of color glazes, ending with a
white glaze to suggest the fuzzy wings and body.
Enhance the delicate details.

Wings may be unusually shaped.

Bodies may be more intricately patterned than the wings.

3
ADD
airholes and other anatomical
features and details.

| 13 | 15 | 5 |
| 19 | 1 | 14 |

Color mix reference chart is on page 17.

Hornets & Wasps

WASPS HAVE TINY WAISTS AND LONGER WINGS THAN BEES. WITH THEIR SLIMMER BODIES AND LEGS THAT TRAIL IN FLIGHT, THEY APPEAR MORE GRACEFUL THAN THE CHUBBY BEE. LIKE BEES, THEIR YELLOW-AND-BLACK COLORING WARNS OF THEIR STING.

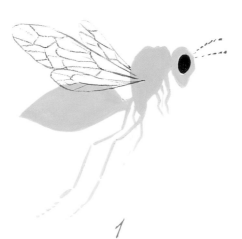

1
UNDERCOAT
the wasp with yellow and black.

2
APPLY
gel medium and blend in shading.

The wasp uses its antennae to measure dimensions when building a nest.

The nest is built by the queen from chewed wood fibers, one envelope at a time.

Hornets are large social wasps, either yellow and black or white and black, that live in colonies

Wasps have long abdomens, segmented antennae and wings placed over the back when they're at rest.

3
OVERPAINT
with distinctive black markings.

4
EMBELLISH
with highlights and fine hairs.

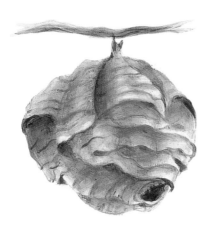

Nests may reach the size of a basketball
and are used for only one season.

A tiny wall wasp might be mistaken for a bee,
but the "wasp waist" tells us otherwise.

Unlike most other wasps, mud daubers are solitary
insects. You'll never see a swarm of mud daubers.

Color mix reference chart is on page 17.

Milkweed & Sumac

MILKWEED IS A DIETARY STAPLE OF QUEEN AND MONARCH BUTTERFLIES. THE SAP'S POISON IN THEIR BODIES DISSUADES PREDATORS. SUMAC PROVIDES ABUNDANT COVER AND FOOD FOR ALL TYPES OF WILDLIFE. BOTH ARE PRIME PAINTING SUBJECTS IN AUTUMN.

1
ESTABLISH
the basic form with light browns.

2
BLEND
in some rudimentary darker shading.

1
UNDERCOAT
red leaves with yellow.

1
POUNCE
in reds lightly with a tiny mop.

3

ENHANCE
and then freehand random seeds.

2

OVERPAINT
with a glaze of transparent light red. Then shade
and add details with a no. 20/0 liner and inky paint.

2

CONTINUE
to shade. Dip a lift-out tool in color and then press
to indicate berries. Apply color glazes and add details.

35	6	21
9	6	29
39	6	40

Color mix reference chart is on page 17.

Spiders & Crickets

SPIDERS AND CRICKETS CAN ADD VISUAL INTEREST. A CRICKET PLACED IN A PILE OF AUTUMN LEAVES CAN MAKE THE ENTIRE DESIGN SING. SPIDERS, IF SMALL AND UNTHREATENING, ADD A SENSE OF MOVEMENT AND DRAMA. WEBS ARE INTRIGUING AND BEAUTIFUL

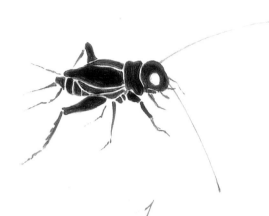

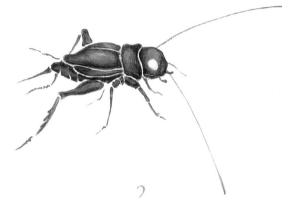

1
CREATE
a sharp-edged dark brown undercoat
with tiny brushes.

2
APPLY
gel medium and blend tan,
white and yellow highlights.

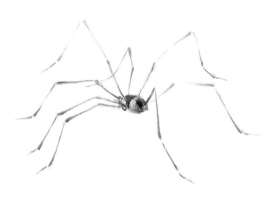

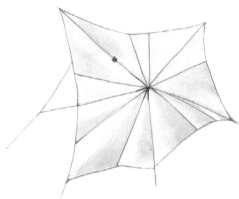

Friendly daddy-long-legs are simple and elegant. They are easily recognizable with their low-slung bodies and lack of waist.

All spiders spin silk, but only some species weave webs.

The web is tethered and a nonsticky framework is added.

Unlike insects, spiders have no separate head. The head and thorax are one, with eight legs attached. The suspended abdomen is separated by a distinct waist.

All spiders have multiple simple eyes. Eyes are larger in hunting spiders who do not build webs to catch prey. Protrusions which appear to be eyes are jaws.

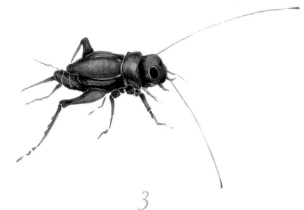

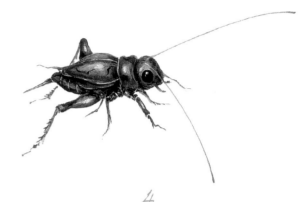

3

ESTABLISH
deep shadows with black.
Blend in with gel medium.

4

ADD
details one layer at a time.
Enhance with hard reflections.

Temporary spirals are added for stability
but removed later.

Many sticky spirals are diligently
woven in the framework.

"Arachnid" means jointed foot. Spider
legs are anatomically like insect legs.
Painted in any position, spiders are intricate
mini-compositions unto themselves.

Hard and shiny or soft and fuzzy, spiders
exhibit a vast array of sizes, shapes, patterns
and colors. All spiders are predatory, but
only a few are harmful to man.

Color mix reference chart
is on page 17.

Woods & Forests

Trees and stones will
teach you what you can never
learn from the masters.

—Saint Bernard

Limbs & Twigs

DEPICTION OF TREE LIMBS, LIKE GRASS, IS GREATLY IMPROVED BY MORE ACCURATE OBSER-
VATION. THESE FEW VITAL BITS OF INFORMATION WILL HELP IMPROVE YOUR ABILITY TO
PAINT TREES AND BRANCHES, WITH OR WITHOUT LEAVES.

Limbs grow in either zig-zag or straight patterns.
Most are straight with opposite branches.

New growth on trees becomes progressively
smaller than previous growth.

Some species exhibit only a few limbs.

Others have innumerable branches and twigs.

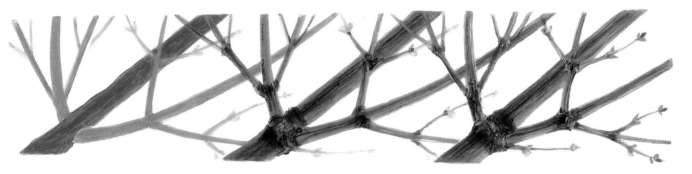

The new growth on branches is always lighter and may be of a different color. Observe leaf nodule patterns and the way branches of various species connect to the trunk and to each other.

Look for attached objects, such as berries . . .

. . . or thorns, to add interest to your painting.

Color mix reference chart is on page 17.

Bark

THE BARK OF TREES IS AS VARIED AS LEAVES. BARK COLOR AND TEXTURE VARY NOT ONLY WITH SPECIES, BUT WITH LOCATION, AGE AND WEATHER. REALISTIC BARK IS EASIER TO PAINT THAN YOU MIGHT ASSUME, IF YOU BEGIN WITH A BASE OF SPONGED COLOR.

1
APPLY
gel and tap in mottled colors with a small sea sponge.

2
ESTABLISH
the pattern of the bark with darker shading.

Smooth bark with horizontal patterns is unusual.

Scaly bark is common.

Furrowed bark is also abundant.

3
ENHANCE
patterns and roughly indicate white highlight areas.

4
APPLY
a series of color glazes. Add details with a liner.

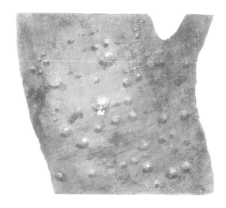

Some species of trees exhibit very warty bark.

Papery or shaggy bark is less common.

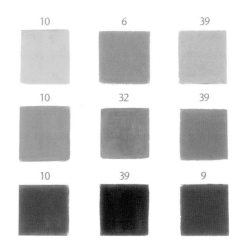

10	6	39
10	32	39
10	39	9

Color mix reference chart is on page 17.

Lichens & Moss

LICHENS AND MOSS ADD COLOR AND TEXTURE TO PAINTINGS OF ROCKS AND TREES. HUMMING-
BIRDS USE BOTH FOR MINIATURE NESTS. AN UNDERSTANDING OF THEIR STRUCTURE GREATLY AIDS
THE ABILITY TO DEPICT THESE INTRIGUING SHADE ORGANISMS.

1
BEGIN
with a gray-green undercoat.

2
APPLY
gel medium and blend shading.

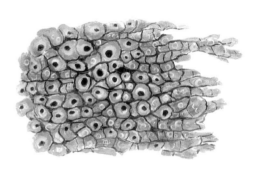

Lichens may resemble tiny trees . . .

. . . or appear cratered and crusty . . .

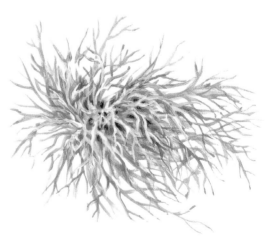

Moss may resemble diminutive forests, . . .

. . . animal antlers . . .

3
HIGHLIGHT
with a tiny mop brush.

4
TAP
in texture. Embellish with frills.

. . . or even have a leaf-like structure.

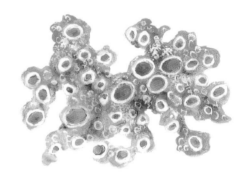

Wet lichens have more intense color.

. . . or delicate, feathery colonies of fern.

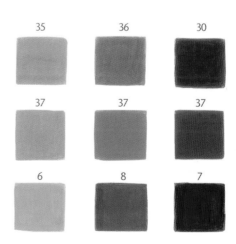

Color mix reference chart is on page 17.

Oaks & Acorns

OAKS ARE THE MOST WIDESPREAD TREE IN NORTH AMERICA. THE WHITE OAK FAMILY HAS ROUNDED LEAF LOBES, WHILE THE RED (OR BLACK) OAKS HAVE SHARP, POINTED LOBES. TREES MAY HYBRIDIZE WITHIN A FAMILY, AND LEAVES CAN VARY UPON A SINGLE TREE.

1
UNDERCOAT
with light-value green and tans,
maintaining sharp edges.

2
APPLY
gel medium. Blend in shading and
set the acorn cap pattern.

Acorns may be short to long . . .

. . . and may have close, tight scales . . .

. . . or loose protruding scales, . . .

Red oaks prefer moister areas. Their leaves have sharp lobe tips that funnel off water drops.

The sinuses between the lobes may be deep or shallow.

3
HIGHLIGHT
with lighter values and paint cap scales
with a no. 5/0 round.

4
FINISH
detailing and enhance with multiple
transparent color glazes.

. . . be tiny with shallow caps . . .   . . . or large with deep caps . . .   . . . or fat with messy, fuzzy caps.

Some oak leaves are atypical, but the acorns are a giveaway.

Color mix reference chart is on page 17.

Autumn Leaves

GLAZING CAPTURES THE VIBRANT COLOR OF AUTUMN LEAVES. NO MATTER WHAT THE LEAF COLOR, ALWAYS BEGIN WITH A WHITE UNDERCOAT OVERPAINTED WITH YELLOW. THIS PROVIDES THE ILLUSION OF MORE LUMINOUS COLOR, BE IT YELLOW, ORANGE OR RED.

1
BASE
orange leaves with deep yellow.

2
ESTABLISH
the growth pattern methodically.

1
BASE
yellow leaves with an intense yellow.

2
SHADE
to establish the form and vein structure.

1
BASE
red leaves with yellow or yellow-orange.

2
INDICATE
veins and intensify the color with glazes.

3
NOTE
that most veins stay green for a period of time.

4
ADD
a series of color glazes. Then add details.

3
BEGIN
color changes away from the vein.

4
GLAZE
in reflections on shiny or wet leaves.

3
DEEPEN
with many transparent glazes of color.

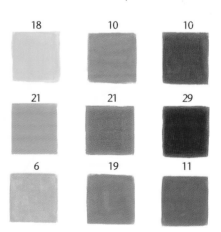

Color mix reference chart is on page 17.

Box Turtles & Snails

SOME BOX TURTLES LIVE TO BE A HUNDRED YEARS OLD. MALES HAVE RED EYES. THEIR SKIN AND SHELLS GIVE ARTISTS THE OPPORTUNITY TO DEPICT A RANGE OF INTRICATE PATTERNS AND TEXTURES, FROM WRINKLED AND DULL TO SMOOTH AND SHINY.

1
UNDERCOAT
with greens and browns. Transfer the pattern
lines and paint the eye.

2
SHADE
the forms and establish the darker elements
of the skin and shell pattern.

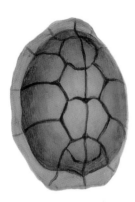

Box turtles share a
basic shell structure.

Varieties are identified
by shell patterns.

Most varieties are distinctive
to a territory.

Box turtles have "beaks," leathery skin
and feet that often appear to be backward.
Old turtles have smoother shells.

1
UNDERCOAT,
shade and highlight the basic snail form. Snail shells
are composed of a lip, an apex and a whorl. The longer
horns are the eyes; the shorter horns, the feelers.

3
IMPROVE
the highlights and shadows with a series
of dark and light glazes.

4
PERFECT
the form with glazes and detailing,
including white shell reflections.

Shells are brownish
with gold markings.

Most box turtles are 5" to 6"
(13cm to 15cm) long.

The young exhibit large necks
and heads in proportion to their shells,
which do not close until the turtle is
four to five years old.

2
ENHANCE
with a series of color glazes and perfect
the details. Snails have no sex, and the babies
look like miniature adults.

| 14 | 1 | 20 |
| 4 | 5 | 5 |

Color mix reference chart is on page 17.

Toads & Salamanders

TOADS USUALLY HAVE DRY, WARTY SKIN. THEIR LEGS ARE SHORTER THAN FROG'S AND WELL-ADAPTED FOR WALKING AND HOPPING. TOAD FEET ARE LESS WEBBED THAN FROG'S BORN IN WATER, TOADS TEND TO RESIDE IN A PERMANENT LOCATION ONCE ON LAND.

1
UNDERCOAT
in dark tan. Precisely transfer
the interior pattern lines.

2
ESTABLISH
the eye, ear disc and dark brown markings.
Moisten dry paint with gel medium and shade with dark brown.
Then highlight with white.

Spadefoot toads have smooth skin
and vertical pupils.

Other varieties have wartier skin
and horizontal pupils.

Salamanders are harmless creatures with wide variation in size, shape and skin patterns.
They have shiny patent leather skin and require a damp, dark environment.

Creature encounters always
make interesting subjects.

3
CREATE
warts by dipping the pointed tip of a rubber wipeout tool in white or brown paint and then pressing it onto the surface.

4
REFINE
the form and skin with a series of color glazes. Perfect the details.

Not all toads are brown
(nor all frogs green).

Toad babies are very tiny, plump and ugly but, nevertheless, endearing.

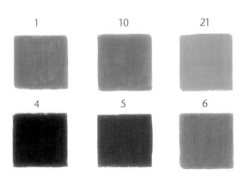

Color mix reference chart is on page 17.

Mushrooms

MUSHROOMS GROW IN A REMARKABLE VARIETY OF SIZES, FORMS AND COLORS—A MUSH-
ROOM TO FIT ANY ARTISTIC COMPOSITION OR COLOR SCHEME! WHILE MOST MUSHROOM
PREFER DARK, DAMP ENVIRONMENTS, SOME APPEAR AS IF BY MAGIC IN OPEN AREAS.

1
UNDERCOAT
the caps and stems. Rough in gill angles
and curvature pattern.

2
MOISTEN
with gel medium and shade with browns.
Enhance the gill shading.

Mushrooms may grow in clumps, . . .

. . . appear diminutive and fragile, . . .

. . . possess unusual shapes, . . .

Not all mushroom families have gills.

Veiled mushrooms retain remnants of
the veil on the cap.

Some mushrooms are devoid of color
and appear ghostly.

3
REMOISTEN
with gel and blend in white highlights. Shade the back side of the gills with the undercoat color.

4
REFINE
with a series of glazes and detail with a liner. Gills in the line of sight are more widely spaced and shadowed.

. . . show very bright color . . .

. . . or show unexpected color . . .

. . . and are always amazing.

These shelf mushrooms resemble turkey tails.

Color mix reference chart is on page 17.

Pinecones

ALL NEEDLE-LEAFED TREES HAVE CONES. CONES ARE THE FRUIT OF THE TREE AND MAY VARY IN LENGTH FROM ½" (13MM) TO 10" (25CM). CONES TAKE TWO YEARS TO MATURE. BOTH LARGE, MATURE AND SMALL, IMMATURE CONES ARE FOUND ON THE SAME TREE.

1
UNDERCOAT
precisely the segments with light and dark brown.

2
SHADE
roughly the interior of the cone with very dark brown.

Pinecones vary greatly. White pine cones are long and loosely packed when mature.

Most cedar cones are tiny and delicately petaled.

Immature bracts are light and hug the core tightly.

The cone will open with maturity and disperse seeds.

In some species, the bracts are papery and flaky.

3
PERFECT
all shading and highlighting using a no. 20/0 script liner.

4
APPLY
multiple glazes of color for a softer, more natural look.

All true fir cones sit upright on the tree branch
and disintegrate to a standing spike.

Some fir cones are very compact with pointed bracts.

More patience than skill is needed for painting cones.

Color mix reference chart is on page 17.

Pine & Spruce

NEEDLES ARE THE LEAVES OF MOST EVERGREEN TREES. NEEDLES EXHIBIT AS MANY DISTIN GUISHING CHARACTERISTICS AS DO THE LEAVES OF DECIDUOUS TREES AND REQUIRE OBSERVATION TO DIFFERENTIATE BETWEEN THE SPECIES.

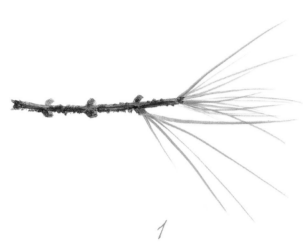

1
PAINT
the pine branch and basic needle cluster nodules. Establish the form of the tip cluster needles. Paint clusters of the appropriate number of needles.

2
CONTINUE
filling in the basic clusters. For exquisitely tapered tips, gradually and evenly ease the pressure on the liner as you approach the end of the stroke.

All pine needles are flat, but occur in many lengths. Some species are extremely short.

Pine needles grow in clusters of two, three or five. Some speci have densely packed clusters while others are sparse.

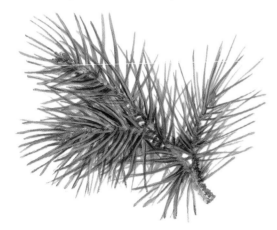

Spruce needles grow along the limb, not in clusters.

Most spruce needles are bluer in color than pines.

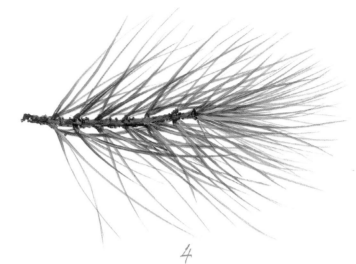

3

SHADE
and embellish the branch. Augment the tip cluster.
Brush-mix color as you work to create automatic shading
and highlighting of needles.

4

ADD
as many needle clusters as needed to define
the species of pine you are painting.
Perfect the shading.

It is essential to pull all pine needle
strokes with a stiff wrist and with your
shoulder guiding the stroke.

Long-leaf pines have needles up to 18"
(46cm). Pine needles are springy, slightly
curved, tapered and graceful.

All spruce needles are
four-sided, stiff and sharp.

Some varieties are very dense and
have an upward curve.

Color mix reference chart
is on page 17.

Cedars, Firs & Evergreens

CEDARS ARE PRICKLY AND HAVE MULTIPLE BRANCHES OF SCALY NEEDLES. FIRS RESEMBLE SPRUCE, BUT ARE READILY IDENTIFIED BY THEIR UPRIGHT CONES AND SOFT NEEDLES. DISTINCT CHARACTERISTICS MAKE OTHER EVERGREENS EASILY IDENTIFIABLE.

1
ESTABLISH
the basic skeleton of the branch.

2
CREATE
tiny scales with a no. 5/0 round brush. Heavily load the brush with yellow-green. Then tip with dark green.

Yews have irregular flat needles and red berries.

Hemlocks bear cones at the tips of the branches.

Fir needles are bluish and display a silvery underside.

Some species dramatically curve upward to the sun.

3
ADD
auxiliary needles of brush-mixed color.

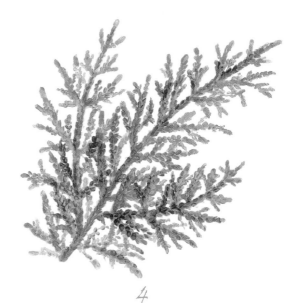

4
CONTINUE
adding needles until the desired effect is reached.
Shade and highlight with brush-mixed color.

This cedar with blue berries is commonly called juniper.

This is the real juniper, used for food and alcohol flavoring.

The fluffy Frazier fir makes a popular Christmas tree.

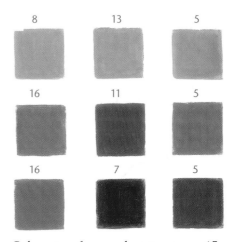

Color mix reference chart is on page 17.

Ivy & Shade Lovers

IVY AND OTHER SHADE-LOVING PLANTS, SUCH AS TRILLIUM AND JACK-IN-THE-PULPIT, ARE FASCINATING STUDIES IN GREEN. GLAZING IS A QUICK AND EASY METHOD OF OBTAINING AN INFINITE VARIETY OF VALUES AND HUES OF GREEN.

1

UNDERCOAT
with dark green, preserving the crisp edges.

Blue-greens imply cool, shady places.

Young plants are a vivid yellow-green.

2
MOISTEN
with gel medium and blend shading with a mop.

3
BLEND
in highlights. Then add glazes, veins and shine.

Intense highlights stand out in shade.

Many species have variegated leaves.

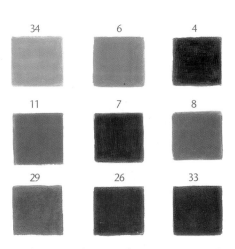

Older plants develop burgundy markings.

Color mix reference chart is on page 17.

Violets

VIOLETS ARE SELF-HYBRIDIZING, SO ALMOST ANY DERIVATION IS POSSIBLE. ALL HAVE DIS TINCTIVE NODDING FLOWERS THAT HANG PENDULOUSLY FROM THEIR STEMS. SOME ARE SOLID COLOR WHILE OTHERS ARE BICOLORED OR SOLID WITH CONTRASTING VEINS.

1
UNDERCOAT
green leaves, blue flowers and tan stems.

2
SHADE
the flowers with purple and the stems with dark brown.

Violets may have deeply segmented and ruffled leaves.

Most common violets have scalloped, heart-shaped leaves

Many varieties bear leaves and stems on the same stalk.

A lance-leafed violet bears flowers and leaves on separate ste

3
MOISTEN
the dry painting with gel medium and highlight the
flowers with white and the leaves with light green.

4
CONTINUE
to adjust the colors, highlighting and shading with a
series of glazes. Spark with bright yellow stamens.

Depict flowers as pale, vibrant or even two-toned in color.

All wild violets appear to be small, delicate and fragile.

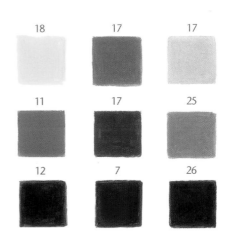

Color mix reference chart is on page 17.

Ferns

FERNS ARE ONE OF THE MOST ANCIENT PLANT FAMILIES. THEY'RE COMPOSITIONALLY GRACEFUL AND USUALLY VERY INTRICATE BUT NOT TOO DIFFICULT TO PAINT IF YOU'RE ATTENTIVE TO THE BASIC FORMS AND PATIENT IN PAINTING THE REPETITIVE LEAFLETS.

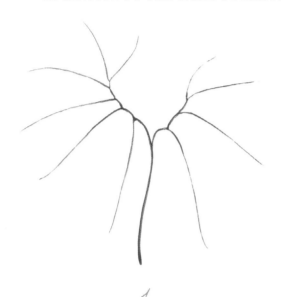

1
PAINT
the dark stems. Purple brush-mixed with brown is superior to black.

2
ROUGH IN
the myriad leaflets along each frond, using a heavily loaded no. 5/0 round.

Ferns offer an endless variety of sizes and leaf shapes . . .

. . . from extremely delicate and fragile with rounded leaflets .

Stems may be green, brown or black; hairy or smooth.

Most ferns, regardless of size, grow in a clump.

3
ATTACH
each leaflet to the stem. Then perfect
the minuscule shapes.

4
ADJUST
the color level of each frond and then shade
with brush-mixed darker greens.

. . . to hardier varieties that propagate from the frond tips . . .

. . . to ones that may wilt but resurrect with new moisture.

Some ferns emerge linearly from the underground rhizome.

Color mix reference chart is on page 17.

103

Ferns, continued

MOST FERNS HAVE TRIANGULAR FRONDS WITH MANY LEAFLETS AND SUB-LEAFLETS. LAYING OUT THE BASIC SKELETON BEFORE PAINTING IS WISE. IF THE TASK SEEMS OVERWHELMING, CUT A FERN FROND, SPREAD PAINT ON IT AND "PRINT" WITH THE PAINTED FROND.

1
ESTABLISH
the basic form of the frond, including the
perspective of the leaflets and sub-leaflets.

2
ROUGH IN
all the leaflets and sub-leaflets methodically,
using a heavily loaded no. 5/0 round brush.

Fern fronds usually produce spores
on the underside.

Some species' spores appear
to be tiny dark stripes.

Other species' spores may have
a fuzzy, rusty appearance.

3

BEGIN
the process of evening out the color levels and
perfecting the individual leaf shapes.

4

CONTINUE
to perfect and then shade the fronds. Haze some
fronds with a glaze of gel and white.

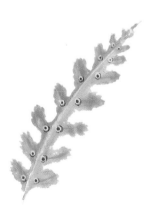

Dots are one of the most common
spore patterns.

Often spore dots are placed
symmetrically on the leaflets.

Color mix reference chart
is on page 17.

Common Leaves

CORRECT SHAPE AND VEIN PATTERN ARE CRUCIAL WHEN PAINTING LEAVES. VIEWERS AR SUBLIMINALLY, IF NOT CONSCIOUSLY, AWARE OF THE IDIOSYNCRASIES OF A PARTICULAR LEAF AND MENTALLY REJECT LESS-THAN-ACCURATE DEPICTIONS. COMPARE THESE LEAVE

Sassafras leaves may have one, two or three lobes.

Some leaves, such as the ginkgo, are unmistakable.

The sycamore has a simple (one leaf per stem) leaf with palmate veins.

Horse chestnut leaves are also palmate, but compound (many leaves per stem).

Leaves, such as the English holly, can be hard and shiny.

Compare the willow leaf, which is very soft and dull.

The leaf of the ironwood has multiple teeth and veins.

This poplar illustrates a simple leaf with opposite veins.

Honey locust leaves are complicated double compound pinnates (many stems of leaflets compose the greater leaf).

Black walnuts exhibit compound pinnate leaves (many smaller leaflets along the stem of the greater leaf).

English oak leaves are hard and shiny and round lobed.

Silver maple leaves are dull and soft with extremely sharp lobes.

Common Leaves, continued

BEFORE PAINTING LEAVES, STUDY NOT ONLY THE SHAPE AND VEIN PATTERN, BUT ALSO THE ANGLE AND CURVATURE OF THE VEINS. LOOK FOR SMOOTH OR TOOTHED EDGES AND TEXTURE. BE AWARE THAT COLOR AND VALUE CHANGE MARKEDLY WITH THE LIGHT.

Painting Soft,
Dull Leaves

1
UNDERCOAT
the fig leaf with a mid-value green.
Accurately establish the edge and vein patterns.

2
BLEND
in darker-value green shading with gel and a mop.
Note the softly fluctuating edges.

Painting Hard,
Shiny Leaves

1
UNDERCOAT
the magnolia leaf with blended mid- and dark-value greens.

2
PAINT
precise, light veins with a no. 20/0 liner. Shade with dark green

The shagbark hickory leaf has large teeth
and relatively straight veins.

Elm leaves have an irregular heel and
many opposite curved veins.

3
HIGHLIGHT
with lighter-value greens. Focus on smooth
transitions from one value to the next.

4
ADD
final vein details with a script liner. Apply multiple
glazes to soften and enhance the leaf.

3
REINFORCE
the shading and highlight with transparent glazes of color.

4
BUILD
gleaming reflections with multiple glazes of white.

The teeth of chestnut leaves are irregular,
shallow, sharp and scalloped.

Color mix reference chart
is on page 17.

Dogwood

THE DOGWOOD FLOWER IS USUALLY WHITE IN THE WILD. HYBRIDS COME IN A RANGE OF COLOR AND PETAL SHAPES. OFTEN PAINTERS PAINT BEAUTIFUL DOGWOOD FLOWERS BUT, SADLY, MISINTERPRET THE LEAF. IT'S ESSENTIAL TO PORTRAY ALL PARTS CORRECTLY.

1
UNDERCOAT
the petals with pale gray-green. Establish the flower center with dark green and yellow.

2
APPLY
a slick gel and begin rudimentary shading and highlighting. Blend with a tiny mop brush.

Hard, shiny dogwood berries cluster at the end of a stem.

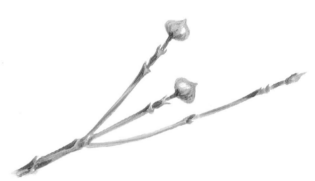

This is a spring twig with opposite flower buds and a growth bud.

1
CURVE
the dogwood lateral veins toward the leaf tip.

2
SHADE AND HIGHLIGHT
the basic form of the veined leaf.

3
CONTINUE
to enhance the shading and highlighting.
Then perfect the blossom with glazes and details.

Red fruits and flowers are not present together on the tree.

3
INDICATE
the subordinate vein patterns for a puckered look.

Color mix reference chart
is on page 17.

Redbud

IT ISN'T NECESSARY TO BE STRICTLY BOUND BY WHAT WE KNOW TO BE THE TRUE COLOR OF A PLANT. LIGHT AND ATMOSPHERE CHANGE COLOR PERCEPTION. HERE, A COOL, MUTED PALETTE WAS SELECTED TO DEPICT THIS SHADE-DWELLING, UNDERSTORY TREE.

1

PAINT
individual spring petals with magentas.

1

UNDERCOAT
with a cool gray-green.

Seed pods darken with age . . .

2
HIGHLIGHT
the base of most of the large petals.

3
ENHANCE
dominant petals in each cluster.

2
SHADE
to establish form and veins.

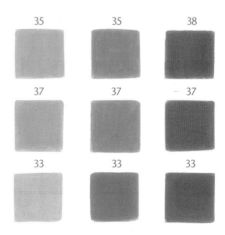

3
HIGHLIGHT
to create a puckered effect.

. . . eventually turning brown.

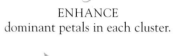

Color mix reference chart is on page 17.

Bird Nests

BIRDS USE NESTS TO RAISE THEIR YOUNG BUT DON'T LIVE IN THEM ONCE THE FLEDGLING DEPART. EACH SPECIES SELECTS TWIGS, GRASSES, LICHENS, MOSS, MUD, SALIVA OR BREAS DOWN TO CREATE ITS OWN UNIQUE STRUCTURE. AVOID PAINTING GENERIC NESTS.

Cliff swallows use mud to build colonies of pot nests on the rocks.

Birds such as orioles and vireos construct hanging nests.

Many waterfowl assemble a sloppy, soggy mess of grasses for a nest.
Though not pretty, it does provide camouflage for the easily accessible nest.

Barn swallows also nest in colonies, with mud and grass shelf nests.

This goldfinch nest uses twigs of a tree for support.

Most large birds, such as hawks and eagles, randomly pile up twigs and branches.
The stack may be refreshed annually and used for decades.

Bird Nests, continued

GEL MEDIUM FACILITATES "BUILDING" A NEST. PROPER BRUSH SELECTION ALSO AIDS IN DEPICTING MATERIALS USED TO CONSTRUCT SPECIFIC NEST TYPES. USE STIFF FLATS FOR LARGE TWIGS AND FLAT GRASSES; TINY ROUNDS OR LINERS FOR MORE DELICATE NESTS.

Coarse Grass Nest

1
ESTABLISH
with inky paint a rough basic form of the nest, including the placement of highlights and shadow.

2
APPLY
an extremely heavy coat of gel medium. Overlay the gel with heavy paint.

Hummingbird Nest

1
DAB
spots of light-, medium- and dark-value paint to create the thimble form.

2
APPLY
gel medium and smaller dabs of color with tiny brushes to blend the colors.

Fine Grass Nest

1
ESTABLISH
the width and depth of the grass bowl.

2
APPLY
heavy gel and paint with reference to light.

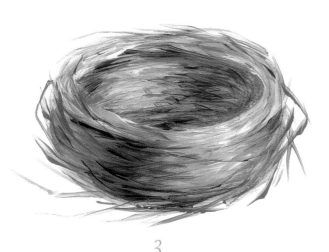

3
STROKE
continuously through the wet gel and paint with clean flat
d/or round brushes, following the lines of the woven structure.

4
REPEAT
the process over and over to "build" the nest, letting the paint
dry between applications. Deepen shadows with glazes.

3
CONTINUE
to apply dabs of gel and color to simulate
the moss and lichen structure.

4
ALLOW
the paint to dry. Then apply color glazes to emphasize
the highlights and shadows of the miniature nest.

3
STROKE
with a script liner to create woven grass.

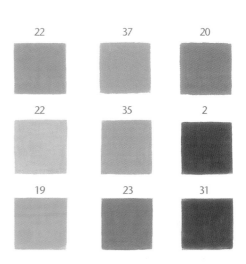

Color mix reference chart is on page 17.

Bird Eggs

REMEMBER THAT THE DEEPEST SHADOWS ON SPHERICAL OBJECTS, SUCH AS EGGS, ARE NEVER AT THE EDGE OF THE SHAPE. ALSO KEEP IN MIND THAT SOME EGGS ARE SMOOTH AND VERY SHINY, WHILE OTHERS ARE FINELY TEXTURED AND LESS REFLECTIVE.

mockingbird

meadowlark

cardinal

Most wild bird eggs are speckled. The eggs of the mockingbird, meadowlark and cardinal appear to be painted with watercolors.

1
BASE
a bluebird egg with bright light blue.

2
APPLY
gel medium and shade the interior. Dry.

3
REAPPLY
gel and softly highlight with white.

Egg size frequently indicates the size of the hatchling, as does the turkey vulture egg seen here.

Some eggs can be incredibly tiny and delicate, as these hummingbird and wren eggs demonstrate.

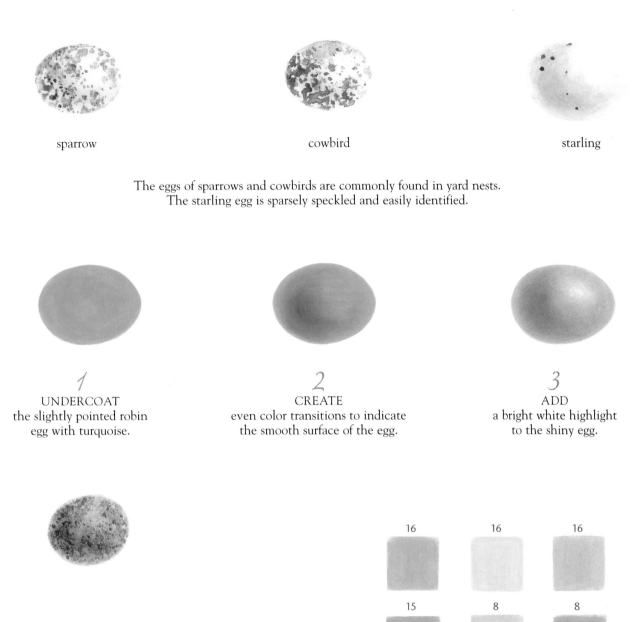

sparrow

cowbird

starling

The eggs of sparrows and cowbirds are commonly found in yard nests.
The starling egg is sparsely speckled and easily identified.

1
UNDERCOAT
the slightly pointed robin
egg with turquoise.

2
CREATE
even color transitions to indicate
the smooth surface of the egg.

3
ADD
a bright white highlight
to the shiny egg.

16	16	16
15	8	8
19	38	28

Unusual eggs, such as pink kestrel eggs, blue-black catbird eggs
and greenish crow eggs, are artistically interesting.

Color mix reference chart is on page 17.

Feathers

BIRDS MAY HAVE FROM OVER 900 TO 25,000 FEATHERS, DEPENDING UPON THE SPECIES.
WHEN WE FIND A FEATHER, WE MARVEL AT ITS EPHEMERAL BEAUTY AND COMPLEXITY.
SOME BIRDS EVEN HAVE ULTRAVIOLET FEATHERS, SEEN ONLY BY OTHER BIRDS.

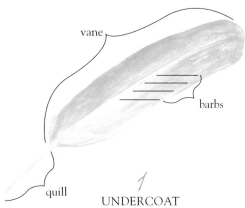

vane

barbs

quill

1
UNDERCOAT
the feather shape with light and dark values of color.

2
ENHANCE
the form with well-blended shading and highlighting.

Intricately patterned feathers are most easily painted with a series of color glazes.
Tail feathers are usually the longest feathers of a bird. As a feather becomes worn,
the tiny barbules, which hold the barbs tightly together much like a zipper,
tend to "unzip," making the feather appear ragged.

Flight feathers are stiff and strong with a narrow vane
on the leading edge and a wider vane on the trailing edge.
Birds also have fluffy powder feathers. The tips of this
type of down feather disintegrate to powder that assists grooming.

3
ESTABLISH
the barb pattern with gel, white and a filbert grass comb.

4
EMBELLISH
delicate details with a liner. Refine with color glazes.

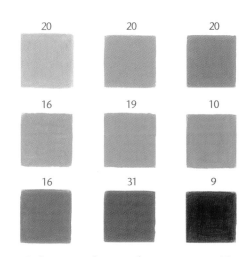

20	20	20
16	19	10
16	31	9

Contour breast feathers are some of the bird's shortest feathers. The vanes are equal in width. Bird feathers grow in feather tracks, interspersed with down feathers. Down feathers, which retain heat, are most numerous on the breast.

Color mix reference chart is on page 17.

Letter to the Reader

DEAR READER,

My sincere wish is that this book will be at your side whenever you paint nature. I encourage you to refer to these pages frequently, not only for creative inspiration and techniques, but also to expand your fundamental knowledge of these commonly painted subjects. The illustrations and text have been designed to help you better see and understand nature, so you will paint nature better, even if you are portraying your subject simplistically.

Keep in mind that there is ample room for variation and artistic interpretation of the subjects seen here. In nature, all species can vary as much as one person varies from another, or one dog from another. However, variance has parameters. We would not think of attaching arms or legs to the head of an animal or person, or placing the eyes on the feet; yet we frequently place incorrect vein patterns on leaves, randomly attach insect antennae or legs and so on. Misrepresentation of these inherent traits can be as disturbing as if we had painted eyes on human toes. My intent is that this book will help you bring rudimentary accuracy to subjects in nature.

Know also that no book or reference photo replaces real models. I cannot overemphasize the value of using life models to elevate the quality of your painting. Whenever possible, place a divot of grass, a leafy branch, a bug or whatever you are painting in front of you as you work. Reality-based observation helps you paint what you truly see rather than what you assume you know.

Finally, to be your best artistically, you must continue to grow creatively, ever striving to improve both your ability to see and your technique to portray your vision. When you think of creativity as the rejection of all the good ideas for the best idea, it becomes obvious that your first ideas are only the beginning.

Best wishes to each of you,

Peggy Harris

the beginning . . .

Resources

GENERAL SUPPLIES

Dove Products, Inc.
1849 Oakmont Avenue
Tarpon Springs, FL 34689
800-334-3683
www.dovebrushes.com
(for painting tools and accessories like sanding pads, sponges, stylus, etc.)

JansenArt Division of DecoArt
P.O. Box 386
Stanford, KY 40484
800-367-3047
www.jansenarttraditions.com
(for JansenArt Traditions acrylics)

Jo Sonja's Inc.
P.O. Box 9080
Eureka, CA 95501
888-567-6652
www.josonja.com
(for Jo Sonja's Artists' Colours, Gel Retarder and Magic Mix)

J.W. etc. Quality Products
2272 Hertz Street
Moorpark, CA 93021
www.jwetc.com
(for UnderCover White Opaque Primer and Right-Step clear varnishes)

Liquitex Artist Materials
888-422-7954
www.liquitex.com
(for Liquitex Acrylics)

Masterson Art Products, Inc.
P.O. Box 11301
Phoenix, AZ 85017
800-965-2675
www.mastersonart.com
(for Sta-Wet Handy Palette)

Plaid Enterprises, Inc.
P.O. Box 7600
Norcross, GA 30091-7600
800-842-4197
www.plaidonline.com
(for FolkArt Artist's Pigments, FolkArt Clearcote Acrylic Sealer and HEATit craft tool embossing dryer)

Silver Brush Limited
92 N. Main Street, Building 18E
P.O. Box 414
Windsor, NJ 08561-0414
609-443-4900
www.silverbrush.com
(for brushes)

Visual Aid Lab, Inc.
2007 W. State Street
Garland, TX 75042
877-960-2923
www.MagnaBrite.com
(for Magnabrite magnifier)

CANADIAN RETAILERS

Crafts Canada
2745 29th Street NE
Calgary, AL, T1Y 7B5
403-219-0333

Folk Art Enterprises
P.O. Box 1088
Ridgetown, ON, N0P 2C0
800-264-9434

MacPherson Art & Crafts
91 Queen Street East
P.O. Box 1810
St. Mary's, ON, N4X 1C2
800-238-6663
www.macphersoncrafts.com

Creative Pastimes Folk Art Studio, Ltd.
235 Bayly Street W, Unit 12
Ajax, Ontario L1S 2K3
905-683-6109
www.creative-pastimes.com

Mercury Arts & Crafts Supershop
332 Wellington Road
London, ON, N6C 4P6
519-434-1636

Town & Country Folk Art Supplies
93 Green Lane
Thornhill, ON, L3T 6K6
905-882-0199
www.artexpress.co.uk

U.K. RETAILERS

Art Express Design House, Sizers Court
Yeadon LS19 6DP
0113 250 0077
www.artexpress.co.uk

Atlantis Art Materials
7-9 Plumber's Row
London E1 IEQ
020 7377 8855

Crafts World *(head office)*
No. 8 North Street, Guildford
Surrey GU1 4AF
Tel: 07000 757070

Green & Stone of Chelsea
259 King's Road
London SW3 5EL
020 7352 0837
www.greenandstone.com

HobbyCrafts Group Limited
7 Enterprise Way, Aviation Park
Bournemouth International Airport
Christchurch, Dorset BH23 6GH
0800 272387
www.hobbycraft.co.uk

HomeCrafts Direct
P.O. Box 38
Leicester LE1 9BU
0116 269 7723
www.homecrafts.co.uk

Visual Index

25

26

27

29

30

31

32

34

35

37

40

43

45

46

50

52

54

55

55

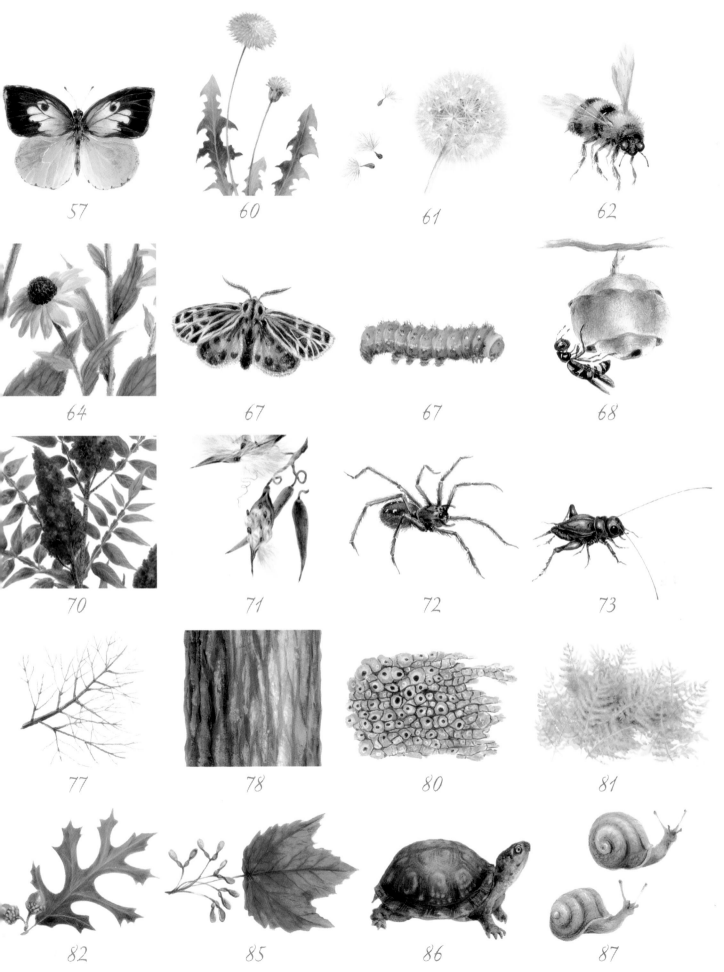

57

60

61

62

64

67

67

68

70

71

72

73

77

78

80

81

82

85

86

87

88

88

90

93

95

95

96

97

98

99

100

103

109

111

113

117

118

121